ECHOES
FROM THE
SCHOOLYARD

ECHOES FROM THE SCHOOLYARD

Informal Portraits of NBA Greats

by Anne Byrne Hoffman

photography by George Kalinsky

foreword by Lawrence F. O'Brien
Commissioner of the National Basketball Association

Hawthorn Books, Inc.
Publishers / New York

ECHOES FROM THE SCHOOLYARD

Library of Congress Catalog Card Number: 77–70140

ISBN: 0–8015–7119–7

1   2   3   4   5   6   7   8   9   10

Contents

Foreword

A book about basketball players written by a ballerina may seem unusual at first, but isn't far-fetched. Both basketball and ballet are exercises of great beauty and grace, and both require performers who possess superior physical ability, stamina, and mental alertness.

Ballerina Anne Byrne Hoffman has a deep appreciation of the men whose stories she tells. But there's a lot more to her profiles than recognition of the players' skills or the fact that she loves the game of basketball.

Ms. Hoffman is a sensitive artist who has the ability to communicate with the inner person. She manages to have each of her subjects look inward and express his feelings about the game and how he became what he is today.

George Kalinsky's photos are familiar to sports fans across the country. His work has appeared in many national magazines and he has collaborated on sports books.

The examples of Mr. Kalinsky's work presented on these pages were selected to complement the mood and character of the stories. In addition to action photos there are many others offering a look at the performers behind the scenes and during quiet, personal moments.

Because of the combined talents of the writer and photographer, I believe everyone interested in the game can gain a new understanding of these outstanding athletes.

Lawrence F. O'Brien
COMMISSIONER OF THE NATIONAL
BASKETBALL ASSOCIATION

Preface

We were sitting in the empty gym of the Bernard Schwartz Physical Education Center of Widener College in Pennsylvania where the '76ers work out. Julius Erving was sprawled on a chair; we were on the floor, looking up. He was smiling, and when asked if he had anything else he wanted to discuss he said yes, that he wanted to talk about the reason for the difference between a performer's need for the audience and the athlete's need for one. He was relaxed and talked freely of memories that had been forgotten for years. And so it went, another interview in another empty gymnasium, another arena in which these men had spent so much of their time. When we left this one at last, Julius said he had honestly had fun talking with us because he had thought about and said things he usually couldn't express in most interviews.

This uniqueness is what we had hoped to accomplish. When we originally discussed our passion for the game of basketball and the men who play it, we realized that our viewpoints differed greatly, yet our feelings toward athletes as artists were more than complementary. As a dancer intimate with the struggle to push a body to almost unnatural physical achievements and a photographer whose emphasis has always been to try to capture the personality behind a façade, we were aware of the motivation that underlies action. Our hope was to encourage these men to reveal aspects of themselves not readily available to their fans by talking about their dreams and aspirations, their drive, their notoriety and fame. The photographs chosen for this book are unusual in that they concentrate more on the personality—both on court and off—than on the players simply as athletes.

So this is, in fact, not our book but theirs—these twenty-four athletes whose levels of achievement have been augmented by public acclaim they first must learn to live with and then must adjust to living without. Here are the men who know what it is to dream and to experience the fight for a goal, a fight that can end with the exhilaration of winning it all or the pain of never coming close.

Acknowledgments

I am most grateful to the men who are the reason for this book—those men who pushed themselves up the mountain confronting their lives and who have told how they feel about the result of that climb and how the walk—or perhaps fall—down the other side looked.

My thanks also to Shirley Dricks, who slaved over static and a subject she knew nothing about, transcribing each and every word; to my dearest friend, Alfonso, who learned a new profession . . . typing, typing, typing; and to my editor, Joan Nagy, for never panicking.

And, of course, to my two children, Karina and Jennifer, who left the bedroom door closed, and Dusty, the man I just love.

Anne Byrne Hoffman

To the players who gave of their time and cooperated with us in many cases under the tight schedule of the NBA season and the emotional stress and pressure of the playoffs.

A special thank you to Eddie Gottlieb, who was so helpful with his vast knowledge of the game and his willingness to share it.

To Dan Gallagher of UPI who supplied us photos of players, taken prior to my being a photographer, that appear on pages 2, 6, 20, 28–29, 44, 53, 61, 63.

To the Public Relations Departments of each of the NBA cities who went out of their way to help not only with the players who are active but were important in the tracking down of those players who have retired.

My warm appreciation to Marty Rosenthall, Herb Schwartzman, Milton Kutsher, and Ed Mosler, who gave their valuable time.

To Lee and Rachelle, who make me so proud, and to Ellen, who makes the sun shine every day.

George Kalinsky

ECHOES
FROM THE
SCHOOLYARD

Joe Fulks

(as told by Eddie Gottlieb)

There was no NBA or BAA in 1945. The Philadelphia Spars, which was my old team, had this program we used to put out for fans who went into the service if they requested it. We had three men in the services in the Philippines. One day we got a letter from one of the fans thanking us for the programs, and enclosed in his letter was a newspaper clipping showing how our players played and how they were doing in the standings. The player who was leading the league in scoring was a guy named Joe Fulks. He was only playing in about half the games but he was scoring all the points. So the next thing I did was write a letter to Petie Rosenberg, one of our Spars over there, and ask him what kind of a player Fulks was. Rosenberg never got the letter because he was coming home on furlough, so when he got home I asked him and he said, "If you can get Fulks we'll win the championship."

Ever hear of Katawa, Kentucky, before? I didn't either. Sometime before Christmas 1945 I wrote to Fulks asking him if he was interested in playing. Later I found out he never received my letter. Then in May 1946 the BAA was organized and I decided to go after Fulks. I called Murray State Teachers College where he went after being discharged. He was not there but they gave me his home number. I told him who I was and he didn't know me from a bag of peanuts, but I thought maybe he had gotten my letter. He said he hadn't. I said, "You know that the BAA has been organized— a big league just starting to play basketball." He said, "Yes." I said, "Would you be interested in playing?" He said, "If the price is right. How much can I get?" At that time we had a salary limit of $50,000 for ten men. One tenth of that amount was $5,000, so I offered him that. The other end of the phone was very quiet and I was thinking to myself, I offered the hillbilly too much money. The hillbilly got back on the phone and said, "No, I can't play for $5,000." I said, "How much do you want?" He said, "$8,000." I talked and fussed around with him but I couldn't move him from the figure. He wouldn't even come down to $7,900. He had $8,000 in his mind and that was it. So I said, "How about coming to Philadelphia? We'll pay for your expenses and we'll discuss this thing in person." He said, "I can't come for a month. I have things to do." Now, I figured nobody knew he existed then, but in a month everybody would know about him and it would really be tough for me to wait that long. I said, "I can't wait a month." He said, "Well, I can't come up before a month." I said, "Will you give me your word that you won't do anything with anyone else till you see me?" He said, "Yes." Before the end of the month Art Morse, an attorney who was running the Chicago club, came busting into the room and said to me, "If you're paying Joe Fulks $8,000 you can have him." I said, "Who the hell told you? We didn't agree to anything with him, but if I can have him, I'll take him anyway."

Fulks came up at the end of the month and I talked a little to him. The first thing he told me was what happened between him and Morse. Morse called Fulks and asked him to come to Cincinnati to meet him. By the time Fulks got to the hotel, Morse was packed and ready to go. Morse said, "Come on, get in the cab and we'll talk going to the airport." When he got into the cab, Morse pulled out a contract, handed it to Fulks and said, "Sign this contract." Fulks said, "We haven't even discussed terms or anything, and furthermore I told Eddie Gottlieb that I wouldn't sign anything till I spoke with him." And he must have told him about the $8,000. Anyway, we talked and talked. I shouldn't say we talked because he doesn't talk. He used to say yes and no, but mainly no—very quietly.

So then I took him out to Pete Tyrel, president of the club, who had to give an okay for the salaries. The three of us got together. You had to know Pete Tyrel. When Tyrel called you on the phone you said, "Hello," but he didn't say anything. You had to carry the whole conversation. He didn't talk and Fulks didn't talk. I had to do all the talking. The end result was that Fulks would not move from the $8,000. He said, "Who you got on the team?" I said, "Well, the only players you know" and I named the players that were there and, "I'm trying to get Jim Pollard." "Oh," he said, "where do you expect to finish?" I said, "One, two, or three." He said, "Well, if you expect to finish one, two, or three and you get Jim Pollard, you'll finish number one." I said, "Is that how good he is?" and he answered, "Yeah." I said, "All right, why don't you cut your demands so that I can give some of that money to Pollard. He said, "$8,000 anyway." I took Tyrel in the back room and said, "Look, we're overpaying him a couple of thousand. We don't know how good he is, *but if we don't give him the $8,000 and he signs with somebody else, and he's as good as he's reported to be, we'll always regret it. So we agreed to give him the $8,000, signed him to a contract, and later he had such a good season that we gave him an automobile for a bonus. Now, he wasn't so much of a hillbilly. Well, I called him a hillbilly. He didn't mind me calling him that. I may have told him later that I thought that I was offering a hillbilly too much money. I'm not sure whether I did. I may have.*

At Murray State Teachers, Fulks was probably a good basketball player, the tops that they had in that area, but he wasn't that well known nationally. Ned Irish of the Knicks made a statement that I had signed the best basketball player in the country. Now whether he knew that the guy existed or why the Knicks hadn't gone after him, I don't know. It looked like the only two who were after him were me and Art Morse. Nobody else had mentioned the fact that they had tried to sign him.

He was married at that time. I'm trying to think if he had one child or two. Anyway, he, the wife and kids I think, moved up to Philadelphia. He had the greatest assortment of shots I ever saw. When he was in the Marines his primary duty was to take care of the gymnasium, and he used to do nothing but stay in the gymnasium by himself and practice all kinds of shots. That's where he picked up all his shots, he said. Left- and right-handed shots—all that stuff he picked up in the gym. I asked him about his shooting and he said he used to practice eight to ten hours a day in that gym. He had to see that the gym was clean, but he had nothing else to do.

In my opinion he had the greatest assortment of shots I have ever seen in a player. Different kinds of shots—one-hand shots, jump shots, right-handed, left-handed, set shots from a distance, driving shots, hooking with the right hand, hooking with the left hand. He was the first jump shooter. They talk about Luisetti. Luisetti was the first one-hand shooter but he didn't jump like Fulks. Another important facet of Fulks was that he was dangerous when they guarded him very closely—two or three men fouling him and hitting him.

People used to say he was a lousy defensive player, which, to a certain extent, I would have to agree with. But I always picked out who I thought

Del Dennis   Joe Fulks   Mickey Vernon

was the best man for him to play. Fulks did not go after the man. He used to put himself in position and the hell with the guy he was playing. At that time he was the best rebounder on our team. I always said as long as he is rebounding like he is, that's defensive work. He's the first player, maybe the only player, that I have ever seen who took a basketball for himself in shooting practice before the game and at half time. Nobody was allowed to take the ball that he shot. He just kept shooting and shooting. The other ones were using four or five other basketballs, and he'd be shooting by himself and practicing all his shots. He couldn't be a playmaker. In the first place he was a forward. Some forwards can be playmakers, but he couldn't. He was a receiver. He had to get the ball.

The night he had 63 points, I don't remember whether he played the *full forty-eight minutes or forty-six minutes. Probably he played the full forty-eight minutes because I had the habit of playing everybody as close to forty-eight as possible. When he got to 63, which at that time was like 125 points today, I said, "You better hang onto that basket and get as many points as you can, because you never know when somebody else is going to come along and beat you." He said, "I don't want to baskethang," and he didn't. He shot better under pressure. On the court he was very aggressive. He used to cuss himself and the referees. He used to talk to himself on the court. He'd be missing a shot and cussing himself and the referees would hit him with a technical because they'd think he was cussing them. It happened two or three times.*

Everybody who ever bumped into him liked him. We got him a summer job with an outfit and they used him as a public relations man, meeting customers and things like that. He was never by himself. He was a good golfer. He played golf on that job. He just met people and played golf all the time.

The bottle. That was the trouble with him. Eventually it ruined him. Especially when we got him that job. I don't know if it was a mistake or not. He also had a habit of getting stopped for passing a red light or going a little over the speed limit. He was always discharged because the police knew him. Everybody knew him; everybody liked him. Evidently he didn't come to Philadelphia as a first-time drinker. He must have been drinking that stuff in Kentucky before he came. He could have played a couple of more years if that didn't take something out of him. I don't think he was built to be a leader but he got along famously with everybody. All the players liked him, and the fans liked him. He was a very lovable character. I don't know if that was the hillbilly in him or what. I don't think the fame got to him at all. I definitely consider him the first superstar in the league. I think he loved all that but he never got a swelled head. He was a free spirit. Free spirits are happy. He wasn't drinking because he was unhappy. He liked Kentucky bourbon. There was only one real problem with him. When I had to negotiate a contract he wouldn't talk. He'd just sit there and listen. The only thing he'd say is no. Now he wasn't so much of a hillbilly.

Max Zaslofsky

In Brownsville, Brooklyn, there were few baskets. We just got those peach baskets and hooked them onto a pole or something like that. And if we were lucky we found a beat-up rubber ball until maybe we could afford fifty cents to go out and buy one, or maybe went to a new school and they had those things in the schoolyard. I loved doing what I did, but my big desire as a youngster, forgetting the monetary end of it, was to be one of the best basketball players that ever lived.

I was always attracted to the game. The first time I had a basketball in my hand I was six years old, and when I was eight or nine I wanted to be a professional player. This is what I always dreamed of and wanted. As a result I spent countless hours in the schoolyards and the playgrounds playing ball—eight, ten, twelve, fourteen hours a day meant nothing. I would rather be playing than eating.

My folks were very, very poor people, but we were very happy. There was an awful lot of love in the family. I have two brothers and there was enough to eat but no luxuries. We never had a nickel or dime in our pockets. So at a very early age I said that sports were very wonderful things; you could make some good contacts and they were a good stepping stone to something else. And because of the fact that we had no money, I always felt if the time ever came when we, or I, ever did have money, I would appreciate it and know what to do with it.

There were few people who were instrumental in developing me; I think I made myself. I never got instructions from anybody. I always played with people who were eight or nine years older than me. So when I was twelve I was playing with twenty-one-year-olds and holding my own. I never wanted to play with a nine- or ten-year-old because I could never learn from him what I could from a twenty-one-year-old. The game was rough and this was how I had to learn. And I had this one desire, to be the greatest basketball player of all time. It was a fantasy, a Walter Mitty thing. That's the dream I had.

The only ball player I saw as a youngster that made any impression on me was a guy by the name of Hank Luisetti. I was a kid, a baby. He came to Madison Square Garden and I went and watched. I watched this man handle himself. I saw how fluid and acrobatic he was in everything he did. *He was from the Coast and was the first man who shot the one-hand shot. It was never seen before. In the eastern area everybody shot with two hands. He was uncanny the way he moved and everything. I was deeply impressed with him. You could call him something of an idol. I had never had any idols. I had never looked up to any athlete; but this man made a very, very deep impression on me. I forget who took me, but I remember we were talking about it all the way back home on the train, and I said to myself, one day I'm going to be as good as Mr. Luisetti, and hopefully better.*

So I participated through high school and into college and when pro ball was born—I'm talking about major basketball—I had just gotten married and was attending St. John's University. A friend of mine asked me if I knew some people who might be interested in being part of this new pro league. I told him I would look into it, and then I went home and sat down and said, if I'm looking for certain people, how about myself. I was only nineteen years old at the time. I contacted my friend and he said, "Well, they are starting practices in Chicago." He made all the arrangements and I packed my bags and went down to a training camp in Chicago which was then the Chicago Stags. Harold Wilson was the coach. I spent three weeks there frightened to death because I had never before really left New York or Brooklyn where I was born and raised. After three weeks the coach came to me and said, "I think I can use you, son. We like what we see out there and you're going to have to speak to our attorney contract-wise." Which I did.

The attorney was Arnold Moss. He asked me if I would be interested in staying there. I said I would if everything were right, not knowing what "everything were right" meant. At this particular point, if he was just going to pay meal money I would have said, "Fine, where do I sign?" So he said, "Well, we'll probably give you a few thousand dollars a year and everything like that." And I said, "That's nice, but how much is a few thousand?" He said, "Well, $5,000." This was 1946. I said, "Fine. Where do I sign?" Now I got pretty smart because it went very easily. So I said to myself, I think I made a mistake by signing for $5,000. I could possibly have gotten more had I been a little more independent. So the following morning I went to his office and said, "Mr. Moss, I'm very happy and thrilled about playing here in Chicago and you offered me a very nice contract. I'm just wondering, would it be possible if I could get maybe $500 more as a bonus for signing, and the only reason I say that is because ever since I was a little kid I wanted to be a professional basketball player, and if I signed a contract I wanted a bonus for signing, so I'd appreciate the extra $500." He said, "Okay, kid, we'll do that." So I signed a $5,500 contract which included a $500 bonus and I have that contract in my house, my very first contract.

I played four years in Chicago. I led the league in scoring in my second year. I had 20 or 21 points a game on the average and the first four years I made all-league first team. Then Chicago folded and the Knickerbockers bought my contract after what I understand was a very grueling session. It's a unique story in sports. Bob Cousy was involved. He had been drafted by the Chicago club, which unfortunately folded the year he was supposed to come. Andy Phillip and I were with Chicago and were up for grabs. The way the story goes, most certainly every club in the league was interested in getting me because of the four tremendous years I had had in Chicago. There were a couple of teams that were interested in Andy Phillip, but nobody was interested in Cousy because they didn't think he would turn out to be a performer. Ned Irish, president of the Knickerbocker club at that time, said, "There's no way that Zaslofsky is not coming to New York City. He's a Brooklyn boy and he belongs here now." Eddie Gottlieb of the Philadelphia Warriors wanted Andy Phillip and me to perform there, but nobody wanted Cousy—so they had a meeting. I understand there was Walter Brown from the Boston Celtics, Ned Irish for the Knicks, and Eddie Gottlieb for the Warriors. The meeting lasted until three in the morning. The commissioner of the league, Maurice Podoloff, said, "Gentlemen, we're getting nowhere. Everybody wants Zaslofsky, nobody wants Cousy, and a couple are interested in Phillip. The only way we're going to satisfy everybody is to put the names in a hat and pick." So they did that and Ned Irish, the first one, picked my name. From what I understand he was joyous, he was stomping and saying, "I got him, I got him." Eddie Gottlieb was the second and he picked Andy Phillip. He was very happy. And that left Bob Cousy. Walter Brown said, "I don't want Cousy." and Podoloff said, "Well, Mr. Brown, you're left with Cousy. There's nobody else left. You have to take him." So, disgruntled and arguing, he took Cousy and, of course, everything after that is history.

I always felt that the athlete was just a vehicle for the owners. I played ten years in a league and the first season when I went to Chicago—nineteen years old with my $5,500-a-year contract with the $500 bonus— was the last season that I attended a training camp. In those years there were certainly no attorneys and business managers like you have today so the ball player had to argue with the owner of the club about salary each and every year. You really couldn't argue much because there was no other league. We dealt with people who said that you played for x amount of dollars and if you said, no, I'm worth more, the finality was, Play for x or don't play. There was nothing you could do. I know it was unusual for me to miss training camp, but for nine years I missed it because I was holding out for more money. I wanted more money because I was productive for the team. And I think possibly it was my background. I could appreciate that the clubs weren't making money then, but I said to the owner, you will be at this game long after I'm finished with it. I only have a few years to be really productive and earn the so-called top dollar. So I have to get as much as I can while I am performing, because the day I start to slip that's the day you're going to start cutting my salary or trade me or fire me. We got into many hassles and I held out every year. As a youngster I learned that nobody is giving you anything unless they feel you deserve it. There are no bargains in this world and you get nothing for nothing.

I'm often asked if I wasn't born twenty years too soon. My philosophy in life is a very simple one. I'm concerned with anything I can control. What I can't control, I don't think about. Now, I couldn't control being born twenty years earlier than when the money came around. If I could, I'd be annoyed or something. But when I played I certainly got paid well, considering the times and tax structure and that you kept most of your money. So it was fine and the monetary end of it wasn't really important *to me until I became a professional. In those days they had many eastern leagues that I could have played for—maybe five or ten dollars a game— and I thought that would be the highlight of my career. So when the BAA and pro basketball were really born and I did sign a contract— well, that was the ultimate. There was nothing for me other than to go out and prove myself to the world, because at that time it was still important for me to have everybody in the world hear my name. I don't know what I had to prove, but I was a nineteen-and-a-half-year-old kid and it was important that my name appear on a marquee. It was important for me ego-wise to see that name up there. That's what made my day. But as I went along through the hard knocks, I saw that professional basketball—and you have to love it to do it, there's no question about it—becomes a very difficult job. The satisfaction of being the best, one of the best, at what you're doing is what gives you pleasure.*

You're conscious of performing in front of x number of people and knowing their appreciation by the applause, but I don't think you hear it nor do you look for something like that. The difference between an athlete, although he's an entertainer to an extent, and the artist, the actor or stage player if you will, is that the athlete will receive the applause from the fans watching because of the nice things that he does. The actor lives for the applause to a degree. I was thrilled by the audience. If I was performing for twenty-five thousand people I was happy, happier than if I was performing for five hundred people. It would excite me more because there was enough ham in me and enough of an ego to get my adrenaline going when I saw a full house. But the fans only see the ball going through the hoop and that's it, because they don't have a full understanding of the mechanics of the body or the individual and what's going on in his mind. It's a private club when it comes to what is performed on the floor. I'm talking about the physical aspect of the game. I can go out and see a dancer and to me it looks beautiful. But someone who is a dancer can pick out finer points and would get more of a kick out of it than I because they understand it much better. It's the same thing with the athlete.

I've watched Julius Erving many, many times and he's poetry in mo-

tion. To watch him and see what he can do with his body—it's fantastic. But people don't see the years spent in working up to that point. It's something you have to live within yourself. I can remember as a youngster the grueling hours, whether it was summer or winter, working on a certain thing, maybe five or six hours a day on a particular move. But the public—not that they should be interested—only sees the finished product. It's difficult for me to try to explain it to people when they ask, because they've never been there. If you've been there, then we're on the same wavelength. Then you can appreciate what I'm saying. Other than that, you're just listening to something that I'm telling you. When the athlete's performing and he does something that the average person may take for granted but there's a little something that's one iota different from the night before, that's when the chuckle comes out.

Nobody knows better than a performer if he's giving 100 percent and if he's doing the best that he can possibly do. My feeling was that I was never really very much concerned with what the audience felt about my performance: I was more interested in my own criticism than that of the fan in the stands. I knew if I was really doing the job or if I happened to be off on a certain night, and that's really where it was at. I was always critical of myself because as I said, I could have always done better.

Each and every one of the players I performed with knew if we were doing the things we were supposed to do, if we were up to par and really using our capabilities. That was the only thing that was important. I couldn't care less if a guy came down from the stands and said, "Max, you had a great game" or "Max, you had a bad game." I didn't even hear him. I wasn't even interested. I thought, you paid your two dollars, fine. You have an opinion. You enjoyed my performance or you didn't. It didn't mean anything to me what the outside world said about my performance. The good notices I got—the press and the media that were excellent—didn't mean much to me. I would rather hear praise from my teammates. When my own peers could say that Max Zaslofsky for the year so-and-so was the best athlete in the entire city of New York— coming from them it meant everything in the world. If they had a vote in the audience and I won, I would be flattered and my ego would be built

up and so forth. But when I'd get it from my own people, then it meant everything in the world to me. I don't see how you can perform without having an ego.

Two of my most glorious moments in basketball were in 1952 when they had a night for me at Madison Square Garden. I was the first New York player ever to have an evening in his honor. And the other, to top it off, was that they had my name on the marquee. This was my dream, that my name would appear on the marquee of the old Garden. Zaslofsky night. I was on cloud nine. My mother and father and my wife came out to center court. It was a dream fulfilled and that's it. You feel good about something like that. My peers did certain things for me because maybe I was good enough. I felt that I was tops at doing something I always strived for. So part of my dream had been realized. The other part of my dream was to make sure that I had enough dollars to take care of my family properly, where hopefully there would never be any want for anything. There has to be fulfillment in everything you do. As a basketball player I can't honestly think of anything I haven't gotten from it.

The only thing I found frustrating was when I left the game. I think I prepared for it, and it was always in my mind. I always thought, I don't know how long I'm going to play—ten, twelve, fifteen years if I can. But if I can play ten years and stay healthy and so forth, I think I can have enough money so I'm not really going to be looking desperately for something. I'm going to be fairly comfortable. So after ten years I wasn't quite thirty. And with all the pressure of traveling, living, and playing in the city for six months, then going back the following season—it was a tremendous burden on my wife and two girls. It was really time for me to get out of the game. The frustrating thing was that the money was very good and I could have played for at least five more years, but it was a decision that I had to make. Where would I be in three or four years? I thought, if I go into business now, I may be better off than I will be if I keep playing. Although the money will be better in basketball than it will be in the business world, I know that for the long pull my family will be better off if I go into business. That's why I made the decision to leave.

Well, there was something missing. I missed the participation, putting the ball in the basket, the excitement of the crowd, the feeling of doing what I did best, the good and bad times I shared. The first four years after I left I was really, really in bad shape because I didn't know what was out there for me. I missed the game and I could have come back. As it turned out, I investigated it and I think I would have played another year had the money been right. But it wasn't. I don't know if it was an excuse or not. I wanted to play.

So the plight of the athlete is a very, very frustrating one. It's almost like a disease. I think I stayed away from it as much as I could. I think the thing that hurt me most was the fact that I knew I could perform. At

thirty, watching the fellows who were still playing, who I played with and against, knowing that I could still do the job for five more years—that was something that was unbearable for me; it really was. I'm not really bitter, because the game has been wonderful to me. In the ten years that I played I was very, very happy and gratified with the things that I did attain, the accolades that were bestowed upon me. My ego was satisfied and everything else was good.

After you quit is when the new challenges come in, the new goals you're looking to set. I'm looking to get involved in certain things that I've yet to conquer. For me to go into a place at eight o'clock tomorrow morning and stay there until five and do this the next day and the next day and the same thing day in and day out, I don't think I could do that. I have to see something different.

Some years ago I came very close to writing a book. I was going to title it, Where Now the Athlete or What Now the Athlete because of the frustrations of the athlete when he's through playing ball. The average person will never know. It's a nightmare. You get a high-strung thoroughbred who's skilled to do a certain thing and he does it for a certain amount of time and now he tells himself for one reason or another that he cannot do it anymore. What does he do now? What is he equipped to do now? Very little. That is what the public doesn't see. They see him out there performing, but they don't see what he goes through afterwards. The so-called good-time-Charlie no longer exists, because you're yesterday's news. While you're performing, fine. Leave me a couple of tickets and so forth and so on. You were the hero so you might have gotten something out of it if they had something for you then. But now you're through playing ball; the doors are shut to you. So what does the athlete do? What is the natural thing for him to do? He can call a sporting goods organization and say, "I'd like to become a salesman." If he's lucky he'll get a job.

Then comes the time, a year or two after you've joined them, when your name has dwindled. There are new people on the scene. "Well, you did a very nice job for us, but there's no need for this kind of work anymore." So you've given them two years of your life, opened up new business, and you're out in the streets. Now, where do you go? You're two years older, right? You don't know any more than you did when you left two years ago. So now you call the liquor companies and become a liquor salesman, or a beer salesman, for the leading companies. The same thing happens there, so it's an endless line.

When I left the game I had money and I was in business and out of business. But I found that in applying for a position where I felt I was intelligent enough, I was rejected so many times that the bitterness and anger came out. I see these things every day with athletes. I can go to any number of players who made an awful lot of money and today are penniless, because when they were through performing they knew nothing else. You can't imagine the scars. I knew the day had come when I couldn't play anymore, so although I'm not performing or in any official capacity, it's a question of trying to stay in the game in some respect. So I approach a player, have a conversation with him, and hopefully do something for him in certain areas. Look for new exciting channels to explore, new challenges, whatever they may be.

I'll always love the game, the atmosphere. These are my people and I can equate myself with them because we're on the same wavelength. Nobody's looking to con anybody. But when you leave that arena and walk out into the street it's "dog eat dog" and you better be ready because someone's looking to gobble you up.

George Mikan

In Joliet, Illinois, we played horseshoes, bocce ball, and a lot of baseball. Marbles was also quite a big thing. In fact, people would enter tournaments starting in grade school and would compete against champions from other schools. There was a series of contests and I won. The reward was a chance to go to Chicago to see the White Sox, where I met Babe Ruth. He autographed a baseball for me, which was one of my most treasured possessions. Now it's lost. One of my sons took it and went out and played with it. Tragedy!

My earliest basketball experiences were in our yard. We made our first basket with stakes and a barrel as the hoop. It was about the size of a basketball, so we hung it up on the garage and got a rubber ball from the five-and-ten because no one could afford anything else. I used to play with my brothers and the guys in the neighborhood. We didn't have any basketball facilities in grammar school, so we played in the park. We practiced there or the local high school, but we weren't too good.

When I went to Columbia Catholic High I wanted to play sports but they didn't think I could because I wore glasses. They cut me from the team. So I left Catholic High after my freshman year and went to a school called Quigley Preparatory Seminary in Chicago, where I studied for the priesthood for four years. At that time my basketball training was very sparse. I was on a seven o'clock bus every mornng and didn't get home until about seven at night, so there wasn't too much time to participate in any athletic program.

However, I was seen by De Paul University. They said if I ever left the school and wanted to go to college, they would offer me a scholarship. My asset at that time was just size, not ability. I was a very tall young man. I knew that ability would take training. I decided that I didn't want to go into the priesthood so I took the offer from De Paul.

I really didn't get too much training till my sophomore year, when Ray Meyer came on the scene. He had been the assistant coach under George Keogan at Notre Dame University. I had been offered a chance to try out for a scholarship at Notre Dame during my freshman year. I went, but just before that I had broken my arch. It had collapsed during scrimmage. I tried to run with the varsity team but couldn't perform too profi-

ciently. George Keogan had them throw the balls at my ankles to see how I would react. I kicked more 3-pointers that way than they do field goals. When it was over, Ray Meyer came over to me and said, "George, I would recommend that you go back to De Paul University. You'll make a better scholar than an athlete." He was wrong on two counts.

Then I had a burning desire. It's something that grew. I wanted to become proficient. I wanted to show people that I could excel. When you're tall, you're always fighting a battle of acceptance. Well, I dedicated myself to becoming proficient in sports. I wanted to be good. It was a means to an end for me—a vehicle to help me get an education. I didn't want to go back to the factories.

With Ray Meyer teaching me from the word go, I was used to taking orders. I had a great father so I never had a father complex. Ray was like an older brother, teaching us all phases of the game. He'd explain why you do things, making you realize that by doing them you would become more proficient. He worked many hours with me before training and after practice. He had faith in me. I sacrificed many things. When everybody else was out having a good time, I was working. I had to work to eat; I had to work to get any spending money. I had to train harder than anyone. At first I had to do things that were embarrassing. The coach had me take dancing lessons for poise and ability. They had me boxing. I ran on the track team for coordination.

The question, after graduation from De Paul University, was whether or not I would make it in pro sports. Again, I was told I couldn't make it, and I told them they were wrong. My first pro experience was with the Chicago American Gears. Chicago had what they called a professional tournament every year. The Globetrotters participated as well as the professional teams all over the country. We won the pro title that first year and I was lucky enough to receive the award as the most valuable player in that tournament. It was a great thrill for me.

My primary objective was to win the games; scoring just happened to come. I always tried to give my best, but in pro sports, the better you become, the more money you make. So I started to try to score. While I was playing we switched from the 6-foot lane underneath the basket to a

10-foot lane. When they moved out, they also opened the area more. This was actually put into legislation to try and stop me from being so proficient underneath the basket.

Instead of getting into the habit of doing only one thing, I was able to adjust and learn various moves that made me a more proficient basketball player. I worked hard. When you begin to approach the pinnacle, your opponent is out to best you every game. I don't care if it's an exhibition game or not, he's going to try to knock you off. You have to accept the challenge and go out and do something about it. I gave out my share of punishment too, don't let anybody kid you. I had a little bit of self-preservation, too. Put the fear of the Lord in the other guy and he doesn't hit you as hard.

A great thing happened in New York. We were playing the Knicks and on the marquee of Madison Square Garden it said, "George Mikan versus the New York Knickerbockers." My teammates taught me a little lesson. We got into the locker room and I was the only guy dressing. They all looked at me and said, "Okay wise guy, you're going to play the Knickerbockers. Go play them." They were really razzing me. We had a great team, a lot of great guys.

But your whole life-style changes when you get out of the game. I wanted to practice law so I became an attorney. I was ready but it was hard. I had often heard that you can take the boy out of the game, but not the game out of the boy. You go to see the ball game, you're anticipating, and until you "shed the monkey" you don't enjoy the game. I shed the monkey by coaching for a short time with the Minneapolis Lakers. But I couldn't stand people violating the basic principles of the game, so the end sort of took care of itself. Then I was talked into running for Congress here in Minnesota. I ran and lost my bid for the seat by less than .5 percent. I went back into the practice of law, but being a personalized service with me away from it so long, I lost some clientele. So then I had to go out and find something so I could take care of my family. That's when I joined Sports Illustrated, U.S. Rubber Company, and Wilson Sporting Goods. It took quite a few jobs to recoup what we lost by my being out of business for a year. My experience as a basketball player

helped me, though. I had always felt that if I conducted myself properly and played well, people would remember. I always liked people; I like to sell. I was in demand for that kind of work and that's why I wound up in the travel business. Even today when I call on people they like to talk half an hour on basketball and five minutes on business.

In my business we sell dreams. I know what satisfaction is because my dream was to become one of the best in basketball. Now I try to make other people's dreams come true. I always felt that I was lucky to be able to be what I was. Today people say, "You should be playing now, you'd be a millionaire." Well, now they've taken the kneecap out of my left knee, my ankles were broken and fixed, but I can't straighten either of my arms anymore. So I paid the price. Yet at least I had the chance to play. It was meant for me to play during that era and I played. How can one have any regrets? I'd do it again.

One of the nice things about basketball is all the friends you make. I still get hundreds of letters for autographs. My family has an internationally known name now. It's sort of nice when people remember and when you're listed among the greats of the world. You'd be surprised how many young people now entering the business world remember you and still think kindly of you. Even today when you watch basketball games they show old movies and it's renewed interest. I just think it's fantastic. Well, they took a poll about the first fifty years of basketball and the sports writers of the nation chose me as the best of all. No one's going to take that away for the first fifty years. I'm grateful. I thanked the Lord that he helped me. But the second fifty years? Debatable.

Dolph Schayes

Even though my personality judgers will probably tell you I'm aggressive, I'm not aggressively motivated, a killer. I think I got into basketball because it was the only schoolyard game in New York City. Basically I was introverted and I guess this was a way to be liked and become part of the gang. Being tall, 6 feet 4 or 6 feet 5 at twelve or thirteen, I was always standing out like a sore thumb. Everybody looked at me. I wanted to be liked and to be with a group and I was able to find that on a team.

My parents moved to the Lower East Side in the early twenties; then they moved uptown to the Bronx. It was definitely a lower middle class existence, living in a one-bedroom apartment and, with my brothers, sharing a pullout bed in the living room that was never paid for. When it finally was, it was time to buy another on the installment plan. We didn't have very much at all.

Jewish guys from those years—the twenties till the early fifties—were great athletes because they were involved in their neighborhoods and they were playing ball. It was a way of getting out. I did well because I played the game a great deal. You just played the game and you were good or you weren't. You made the team or you didn't. I was a good basketball player and I never thought of drive. I loved it when I was accepted by my peers as something special. I guess I just wanted to play ball.

I had coaches who were drivers in junior high school, high school, and college. I learned and I did things. When I got into professional basketball I became more tigerish under the influence of coaches and other players. I was a great copier. If there was something I liked, something I hadn't seen, I wanted to be able to do it. I think that helped my aggressiveness, which I needed to become successful. The infighting is close. Also, I had a lot of frustrations, like everybody in everyday life. I don't think I solved them very well, but the court seemed to be an outlet for all the pent-up aggression and frustration that I couldn't release in the everyday world. That, plus a desire to do well, gave me the impetus to succeed.

I didn't have much speed but I felt that by constantly moving I could free myself, so I moved in and out all during the game. I kept pushing myself. I saw myself never getting tired. You can seemingly go on forever. It

was a great feeling to play forty or forty-five minutes, which I did year in and year out, and not get tired. Perpetual motion! A couple of the players called me the Circler because I constantly circled around and made figure eights. We played free-lance in those days and we really had players. I got on a team where I had to play forty minutes a game and I had a coach who was a driver. Perhaps this is why I developed good physical agility.

There's a direct correlation between drive and success in sports. You just have to want success very badly. In many cases winning is great but from an individual point of view there's a fight within everybody, I think. Most people want to excel selfishly; they really do. And if winning comes with it, that's great. But real success is a combination of both personal and team accomplishment. A person can't be a winner unless he's very selfish, and I sometimes wonder which is the more important—the individual or the team effort. Of course, the coach is trying to instill the idea that unless you win you're not a player. I think a player has to be selfish first and then perhaps the coach will turn him into a winner. But players say, "I'm a team player; I love to win." But they really want to excel individually first. I think that was my motive, too. I wanted to excel individually. If I had the ball on the court and there was a guy ahead of me, naturally I'd pass him the ball. But each individual has his own ego to satisfy. It's the coach's job to mold the individual into the team.

I think I enjoyed the adulation as much as anything. Everyone, I think, wants to see his name in lights, read the write-ups, feel like a big shot. I was never really a big shot. Throughout my career I wanted to excel. I wanted to be liked and well thought of and to let out my frustrations. And then there's that tired feeling after it's over; you feel so good when you've done something and you've done it well. Money was never really that important to me. I was one of those guys who felt like a kid about money. Many times I never signed contracts. My main motives in playing professional basketball were to do well, enjoy the life, bask in the adulation. I wanted to play and the game helped my ego so much. And they were paying me!

Then I had an operation and I quit. The operation proved very successful so it bothered me that I had quit. I thought I had a year or two left, so I reacted very strongly to the knocks that came because I wasn't conditioned against knocks. Most times good things happened to me and I was shielded from the bad things. I would say from junior high school through high school and college when I played organized ball, I was always being written up, lionized. I never really had any bumps and smashes. That didn't help me, especially near the end of my career. I had been conditioned for success for twenty-five years and you can't be shielded from the knocks. They should be part of your life. But for some reason that had never been a part of mine, so when the knocks came I just wasn't ready. It really bothered me and I reacted very strongly.

There was a transition period where I had trouble getting away from basketball. I had gone through a myriad of jobs in the summer—engineering, insurance—but there was a constant fear. What am I going to do? Am I going to be thrown out in the streets? I think very few people really do prepare for a future until they finally get out of basketball and get into something else.

Well, I got out of basketball in 1964 after playing in Philadelphia for a year. Then I went to Buffalo as coach, which was a disaster. I pulled the dubious record of being fired after one game of the second season. Of course, this was a jolt to my ego. That took quite a bit of getting over. Then, of course, you rationalize, and say to yourself, what am I, some kind of a child? Grow up! You have to find something else that you can be good at, so that your ego can be strong and you can be fulfilled every day in your workaday life. Eventually I got involved.

I had the impossible dream that I wanted to be the best player in the world—to have people say, "That guy is the greatest," and to have all the records. I wanted to be remembered that way. It's such an impossible dream. I knew I couldn't fulfill it. I knew I was playing selfishly for the adulation. Now I realize there's a great possibility that I took something away from my kids. Today my dream is to have a whole family. I'm trying very hard to make up for those years when, because of my constant fear, I didn't give. Did they have a father? Those years when you're holding the baby, the kids are on your knees, when you're working and playing with them, are lost to me now. Any athlete with a family today should spend time with those kids. Even if it isn't a long time, it should be concentrated, because they'll be scarred for life and you'll miss them.

My kids are great kids and I'll have withdrawal symptoms when they all leave. I hope that I was okay and gave them enough. Today is for them. They should be strong and successful. That's why the second dream is the most important one.

Paul Arizin

In South Philadelphia people didn't have much money. One of the things we used to do was hop trucks. The truck route was very close to us. We'd hop a truck, ride it to Wilmington, then get off and ride back—just for something to do. We didn't have the distractions that kids have today, so sports became our outlet. Our area was not abundant with grass, so we played in the streets. There were no cars parked there because nobody had them. I distinctly remember playing baseball and football on the streets. You had to get involved with something that occupied your time and didn't cost money. Sports were perfect and I liked them. The area was not heavily oriented towards basketball. It was sort of looked upon as a sissy game. In fact, I never saw basketball till I was in the eighth grade when I went to a parochial school that had a basketball team.

The sister who taught us knew nothing about basketball, but she was told that the school had to have a team so she chose those she considered the best students. I was one of the better students, so I was chosen. I didn't have the slightest idea what basketball was all about. My initial contact with the game wasn't very dramatic or glamorous. My whole eighth grade year I might have scored 10 or 15 points.

I was, I guess, a fair-sized kid, not overly big or small, when I went to high school, and I was still playing sandlot baseball and football. At La Salle High School I went out for the basketball team and was cut. Apparently the team didn't miss me very much, because they won the city championship.

In 1947 I graduated from high school and I was probably getting a little bit better. Then a dramatic change occurred. A fellow I started to pal around with didn't like to play baseball at all because of the slowness of the sport. So I started to play a lot of basketball with him. In that summer a lot of veterans were coming back from the Second World War. I was working to pay my way at Villanova, and because of the returning vets I played with a lot of these independent leagues that were set up for the guys looking for an outlet in sports. I was a chemistry major at Villanova and I commuted from South Philly, which is about an hour commute via public transportation. I must have played an average of six or seven *games every night during the season. I played so much I just got better. At the end of the year the team I was with won, and I got the Most Valuable Player Award. So after my freshman year at Villanova I got a couple of feelers from other schools about going there on scholarship. My family wasn't wealthy enough for me to ignore the offer of a scholarship. I was going to leave Villanova, but in one of the tournaments I played in, our team went to the finals against the Villanova team. The guys were primarily freshmen back from the service. I got the Most Valuable Player Award in that tournament. The coach said, "Well, if you stay here we'll give you a scholarship." I liked the school so I said, "Fine."*

In my sophomore year I didn't start the first several games. Then I started with the same fellows I had played against in last year's tournament. I guess I had an average year. We had a pretty good team and scoring was balanced. In my junior year I started to score more. My senior year was my best one yet. All this time I still considered myself a student. I loved sports and the NBA had been formed. I used to go out and watch Joe Fulks and the rest of the Philadelphia Warriors play, but I never had any aspiration for being a pro player myself. In fact, at that point I never had any aspirations about even being a college player. I was sort of in awe of the things that happened to me. I said to myself, gee, this is great. I wonder how long it's going to keep up. The fact that I wasn't good enough to play in high school had left me with the feeling that I wasn't good enough to play in college.

I was very fortunate that the fellows I played with in college were excellent players, but none of them were very good shooters. My forte was shooting so I sort of blended in. I gave them what they needed in shooting and scoring and they really added to my all-around game by their general knowledge and court awareness. I felt that I played with a very smart team at Villanova. From what I've seen in basketball since then, it's not only ability that counts, it's being in a particular place at a particular time when they need your skill. I've seen more good players who didn't make it because they weren't in the right place at the right time.

I graduated in 1950. So did Sharman and Cousy, who were already pretty good players. Eddie Gottlieb exercised a territorial right and picked me first. I guess he had always been inclined to lean towards homegrown players. I think he felt they were a better draw in Philly. The choice was whether he would pick me or Larry Foust from La Salle. Larry was a 6-foot 8-inch center who eventually played eight or ten years

in the NBA and did a good job. Anyway, Gottlieb picked me. I was rather surprised that he did. Well, I decided, let's see what happens. Maybe I'll make it, maybe I won't. If I don't, I always have my education. I still considered myself a student, someone who went to college to earn a living after college. I loved playing sports and if they were going to pay me for playing, I'd wait and see what happened.

When I played that year I had no aspirations, but things went well and I wound up having a very good year in the NBA. I was very pleased. I said, let's see what happens. If I don't do well I can always get a job. We dropped off a little in the second year. A lot of the players on the team were thirty or a little older, having served in the Second World War. Our team was sort of aging so I think they went more to me for scoring. I could do two things very well in basketball and I think they are very important. I could shoot well and I could jump. I happened to get lucky and win the scoring championship. I was a very competitive person by nature. I liked to do things well. In high school and college I was always a good student. I liked to be up there among the best. I liked to play hard. It was my competitiveness that helped me as I progressed. Competing is fun, although it's not much fun unless you win. That's my assessment. Winning is important. I'm not sure that we played really well when we lost because I felt there was always something else you could have done when you lost. I felt that the one objective of being out there was to play well enough to win. If I played well enough to win, I was generally happy. I think even on my best days, if we lost, I probably made several bad plays. You go back in your mind and you say, gee, had I done this differently or had I done that differently the outcome would have changed. There were many times when I felt there was a clear win even before the game was over, and I would have preferred to be out of the game. When the game is over, scoring doesn't mean anything. No sense playing anymore, the job is done. Let the other guys play. I would much rather participate in a close win—a 1- or 2-point game—because I think when you win by a lot of points it's not nearly as exciting a game as when you win a close one. You play as good as you have to play when you win.

Paul Arizin

I don't think I was ever content to accept defeat. I'm one of those guys who has a very difficult time sleeping when I lose. I replay the game over and over. I must have replayed twelve hundred or fifteen hundred basketball games. I think that's just sort of my high-strung nature. Athletics is an area of peaks and valleys. It's sort of a feeling of expectation before the game. You never know; you just wait to see what happens that night. When I played I never enjoyed food the day of the game. I would just wait. In fact, if I had my own way I would have played afternoon games to get them over with.

I was surprised when I dethroned Mikan for the scoring championship. I never thought anybody would dethrone him. He had won it for eight years. The reason it came about, I think, was that Eddie Gottlieb thought it helped the team to have someone who scored a lot of points, so he pushed me as much as he could. Also there were many games when I thought the team needed the points. But I never felt that just scoring the points, garbage time if you choose to call it, was important. Forget it; take me out. Or I just wouldn't shoot. Eddie used to give me hell. But I was very happy and pleased to beat Mikan. I knew I was doing well, and had arrived, and was truly a pro.

To be honest, though, I won two scoring championships and neither one of those was the highlight of my career. I don't rank those nearly as important as, say, winning the championship in 1956. If you ask me what I was most proud of, it would be that. I would have liked to be the player who played in the most winning games and the most championship games. Being on a team that wins the most games, you know you've gotten the job done. That to me is the mark of doing the job well. A reaffirmation of this good job is that everybody contributes to the victory. I think there's a certain element of sacrifice and self-discipline that's necessary for that.

It so happened that one of my principal means of contributing was scoring, but I don't think it was the only way. A heck of a lot of guys who played on the teams with me didn't score nearly as much but were every bit as important in the wins. I've always felt badly to a degree that other guys didn't get the credit they should have. I really think it's a team effort. Where I contributed the most, scoring, was fortunately or unfortunately the area of the game that was the most publicized. I never felt in my own mind that it should have been true. They gave me a lot of praise and maybe in a way I deserved it, but sure as heck a lot of those other guys deserved it too. But they weren't getting it. They were contributing as much to the wins as I was. But you're not going to change the world and you're not going to tell the sports writers, "Hey, you shouldn't write about the guys with the scoring. You should be writing about the other guys." I don't regret having done it the way I did. But as I said, the most satisfying moment I ever had playing ball was winning the championship in '56. That far surpassed any individual honors I have ever received. That was really the culmination.

I really didn't like the limelight. When you went to a restaurant people came over to you. I didn't like that. By nature I'm a very private person. It was especially bad after a lost game when people came over and said, "What happened?" At times like those you feel like getting up and punching them. You feel bad enough about losing and then some guy you don't even know comes up and says, "What happened?" But that's part of the game. I would try to go to places where I wouldn't be recognized, where I wouldn't be known. But you can't do that all the time. You just live with it. You just try not to be rude, try to treat people as you would hope to be treated yourself. You read a lot about athletes saying they miss the limelight, the glamor. Believe me, I don't miss it one bit. The only thing I miss is the game and the competition. Basketball was a phase in my life. Now basketball is over with and I'm into new things. Don't judge me as a basketball player.

When I retired I was playing forty minutes a game and averaging 22 points, so I still had a lot of basketball left in me. But I just got tired of playing. It was not as much fun as it used to be. My body was still in good shape but I couldn't run as hard and as long as I had five or six years previously. I don't think I was losing any of my physical skills. It was more or less a mental decision. The team moved to San Francisco. I didn't feel like leaving the Philadelphia area; I was raised here. The only time I left Philly was for two years in the service. My wife is from this area, too. In traveling the country I never saw a place I'd rather live in, other than the Jersey shore where we go every summer. I still like this area. I think it's *important that my family is here and that my wife's family is here too. I didn't like the traveling, the flying, the being away from home. My oldest child was nine or ten, and I said, heck, this is the time to make a decision. I made up my mind. I can still play but I don't want to go out a bench-rider. I couldn't take going out as an old has-been. Also, I had something to go to—an offer from IBM. I also played with an eastern league on weekends but that began to be like working seven days a week, so I walked away. I have always wanted to leave myself in a position where I can walk away from whatever I don't want to do anymore. That's just what I did with basketball.*

I never had a dream except to have a family, which I now have. Five healthy children, thank God. I never dreamed or expected to be president of the United States or anything of the kind. In my early background there was never an inkling of stardom. I was not an all-American in high school or anything like that. I was in intramurals in high school, so stardom was very surprising. I felt that the ten years I played I earned my money. I enjoyed it. Most people can't claim that. Most people, I feel, don't really love their jobs. It's a limited few who do, so I feel I was very fortunate.

I don't know whether it's good or not, being in any job a few years and being set for life. If that's the case it sort of takes the challenge out of everything. I think in order for there to be a challenge there has to be a need, a hunger. How am I going to support my family? How am I going to earn my livelihood? When you do something to achieve that you get satisfaction. I guess it's the same thing if your father has $90 million, and from the time you're eight years old you never have to worry about money. You can't be achieving a heck of a lot, regarding finances at least. You need another outlet. There was no way, with the money we made, that you felt you were going to be settled for life. You knew that when your basketball career ended you would have to get yourself established in something else which was real. I guess that was a motivating factor in my quitting. I was making pretty good money but I'd be making more than that when I got into business, so what's the sense in waiting around. If there are no obstacles in your path and everything is laid out, you win no challenges. I like what I'm doing. It's challenging; it's an interesting job, but it's not like playing basketball. I don't think I would have liked anything else as well as basketball.

Bob Cousy

My mother was a very, very, high-strung Frenchwoman who fought for everything in her life. My father was very easygoing, complacent, unflappable. I was honed from a combination of the two. Also, I had the fortune to be born a natural athlete. I grew up in the ghetto where you literally had to fight for everything you owned. I think if I had been born into an affluent situation perhaps my competitiveness wouldn't have come out as quickly. I think it was that simple. The basic requirements were there and the environment brought it out. You were forced into using your imagination in those days. Today everything is laid out for you, programmed, and kids hardly have a chance to enjoy growing up as much as we did. In material terms we had very little and yet I don't think we missed much or even recognized that we had it bad. We just had a ball and if we didn't have a great deal else, well, that was fine.

My recollections of my childhood are extremely happy even though I am aware that for twenty-two years my father pushed a hack in New York and finally saved $500 to get us out of Manhattan to Long Island. So things were that tough and yet they were not tough. I don't remember having any great desire for material things. I remember I waited three years for my first bike and that meant a great deal to me. But I never felt deprived in any way. We just grew up normally for those times. We were just average kids putting a little time in school and hanging around the schoolyard every afternoon, doing our thing.

Initially, I was involved with the street games in the ghetto on Manhattan's East River—stickball and box ball, steal the apple from the pushcart, whatever—the type of thing that kids play under those circumstances. I was thirteen when we finally got out of Manhattan and went to Long Island, which at the time was a hotbed of basketball. Almost from the first time I was exposed to basketball I gave up most other sports. Every kid's ambition in the area was to make the local high school team. Other than that we had no unusual ambitions. We didn't have the idol syndrome that kids have today, either, at least as far as basketball was concerned. There was no professional basketball. College basketball was not getting a lot of exposure, so we were doing our own thing.

Basketball fit my particular talents—speed, quickness, peripheral *vision, etc. You thank God if you have these talents, but you don't just ac-quire them as you go along, you have to cultivate them. At the time I was a skinny, short kid and the school I went to had three thousand boys. Everybody wanted to make the basketball team. The coach had such a tremendous amount of material! I guess the first traumatic experience of my life, at least that I can recall, was when I was turned down for the high school team. I made up for it by playing with many outside teams. I used to play, under different names, in three different leagues at the same time. As I say, we were completely immersed in basketball. After the second turndown my sophomore year, I was finally observed playing with one of these outside teams at the local community center where the high school coach happened to be the supervisor. He saw me playing, but even then it was under somewhat unique circumstances. I had broken my right arm ten years before, and with the cast on, I'd had to play lefty. As a result I developed enough confidence and strength in the left hand to impress the coach. When he saw me play, he thought I was left-handed. He just happened to have a position on the team that called for a left-handed shooter. He said, "You're a lefty." and I said, "Well, no." He found out what I was and said, "Well, of course, come out for the team." And that's how I was invited out. It's possible, if he hadn't seen me, that I'd have gone out in my junior year and maybe made it, maybe not.*

Eventually, though, I would have made it, because in my junior year I developed a clear-cut advantage over my contemporaries: an intense, competitive spirit. You can't tell, when you're watching kids in a tryout, if they're killers unless you see them on a sustained basis.

It wasn't until my last year that I was aware that I could use my ath-letic talents as a vehicle to get to college. I had never considered it. It was obvious my folks couldn't afford to send me and I was not a particularly good student. In fact, up to the point when I developed this realization I was a very mediocre student. When I became aware, just prior to my last year, that basketball could get me into college, I simply went to work and my grades improved considerably. I had motivation, so I worked to my full academic capacity my last year. As a result, I was able to go to a good school. This was 1946 and I was all-city in New York, which at the time was a big deal because New York was a very productive area for high school basketball players as it is now for college players. I was deluged by all of two college offers when I got out. A kid who is all-city of New York today would have upwards of four hundred schools and recruiters sitting on his doorstep.

I went to Holy Cross. We were allowed to play varsity as freshmen during the war years, so I played as a varsity member and we won the NCAA, which is the epitome for a small Jesuit school. We just happened to come into a lot of talent at one particular time. I don't even recall when I started to get all-American recognition; probably my junior year. But the point is that I had four good years of sustained growth in terms of ability, exposure, what have you. The pro league started in 1946, the year I got into college. It was nothing to get excited about, as I recall. As a matter of fact, as much as we were into basketball, as much as we were into college ball, we didn't pay too much attention to the pros. The Boston team might have started a year or two later, 1947, '48. I don't know if we even went to see them play. It just wasn't a big deal.

I graduated in 1950. A friend of mine and I were going to go into business together. I knew I could be drafted by the pros, but I made up my mind. I was going to play only if Boston drafted me. They didn't, and I was drafted by some place called Tri-Cities. I said, "What is Tri-Cities?" which didn't endear me to basketball fans there. Negotiating a contract took a long time because I was asking for $9,000 and they were offering me $7,500. I said, "Gee, I'm sorry, I'm not interested. I'm going into business with this friend of mine in Worcester." I remember the team owner thought I was just pulling his chain. I wasn't really sure I wanted to continue on a pro level. Obviously, every kid on a varsity team today wants to play pro. But I was quite serious because, if for no other reason, my friend and I had a great deal of confidence that we could each earn more than $7,500 outside of sports. I hadn't gone to school for four years just to do fairly well. Eventually I got traded to Chicago. Then Chicago disbanded, all our names were thrown in a hat, and I ended up in Boston—which is the only place I would have played anyway. I never moved from Worcester.

Just prior to my coming, Boston had been burned by a couple of kids who graduated from Holy Cross. They had been local favorites and the media insisted that Boston choose them, but they didn't pan out. The priority, then, for an effective basketball team was still the big men: center and forwards. The guards were always more of a gamble. The first six years we didn't do a hell of a lot collectively, but my last seven years we won six out of seven championships. So we all got spoiled and expected that same success every year, which also is unusual. Hell, guys play a whole career and never even smell a championship; some of them never even make play-offs. We were damn lucky, but it also made me more aware that basketball is not an individual sport; it's a game that requires more teamwork than perhaps any other sport, although there is opportunity for individual creativity.

As a player I used to feel that winning was the whole thing, though obviously you want to do well individually. But I used to get more satisfaction out of success as a coach. If you have playing ability and complement it with a mental approach to the games, you get not only great satisfaction but much better control of yourself—in coaching there's less individual control. You put in more work, time, effort, and concern on trying to mold a dozen different personalities. You put all this work into producing a cohesive, unified effort out there among those different personalities, which is tough. The feeling must be analogous to whatever an artist or sculptor feels when he's put all his work into a piece and all of a sudden he's going to unveil it. This piece is him. It's a reflection of his ego.

I used to call myself a sore winner because if the team played badly and we won anyway, I used to be upset. Sometimes, as much as I hated to lose as a coach or a player, playing well neutralized the feelings of losing. As long as the team played as well as it was capable of playing, I could live with the loss. But if the players were sloppy and didn't function the way I wanted them to, then a win was neutralized. When they both played very well and won, that was the ultimate in satisfaction.

I was never a cocky athlete, but I was always very confident of my ability. When I was younger I used to go out knowing that I could do my thing without any concern. Generally, pre-performance butterflies scare the hell out of you until the curtain goes up or the whistle blows. Then you go out and function, scared or not, because you're prepared. Once that whistle blew, I knew I was better than anyone else.

I didn't need any additional stimulus for competition, but when I got older I used to look for things to help light the fire a little more quickly. Particularly during play-offs, if I had not been able to generate the necessary emotion prior to the game, I would go through all sorts of weird rituals. I'm a loner to begin with, but I used to take great pains to isolate myself completely from the outside world for twenty-four hours, if possible. I would have all meals sent up. I wouldn't answer answer the telephone. I would do my hermit bit, simply trying to concentrate on the task or on an individual. I would try to direct my animosity towards an indi-

vidual rather than a team, if possible. I'd use whatever vehicle I could as a stimulus because I felt it was necessary.

Once I started to get older my physical skills started to diminish and a feeling of apprehension began to set in. I knew I could no longer control my destiny. That's when the pressure really begins to accumulate because you know those young kids coming on court have saliva dripping at the corners of their mouths, and they've been locking themselves in their rooms for twenty-four hours to do their number on you. What drove me out of the game eventually, though, was mental boredom rather than any diminishing of physical ability. Obviously I didn't play as well after thirteen years, but it was the repetition, the life-style that drove me out. I guess if I'm honest about it, it's that you start thinking about the pressure and the fact that you're playing a child's game four and a half times a week. You start to get into the self-analysis bit, the what's-it-all-about-Alfie? What are you doing in terms of your priorities and your family?

Suddenly I was thirty-four years old and this child's game had been all-consuming up to that point in my life; everything else had played a very secondary role. My daughters were eleven, twelve, or whatever, and I had spent little time with them. We were almost strangers. Our entire family life had revolved around me doing my thing. Then there was the pressure. You never feel pressure when you're young—at least I never did. The fear is simple. It is much easier to get to the top than to stay there. Once you reach a certain level and your physical skills start to diminish, you still get out there every day but you're tired and not up to your best performance. Yet you're going out and there are fifteen or sixteen thousand people out there, and every daddy is saying to junior, "There's the best basketball player in the world. He's the greatest." And you know that you cannot perform up to that level. It is not necessarily a case of being humiliated, but of just not being able to play to your own standards as well as to the fans' standards. And part of my motive to quit playing was pragmatic. I wanted to quit "on top" so I could capitalize on it for the next twenty years. At today's salaries you can just hang on for another three years and make another million bucks. But at our salaries it became very important, given the level I had reached, that people con-

tinue thinking I had been the best player at one point. If I had stayed around one year too long and miscalculated, all of that would have been down the drain. Referring to basketball as a child's game sounds like kind of a put-down, which it shouldn't be, I suppose. Sports can be an art form like anything else, and if that's your thing and you do it well, you can get as much satisfaction out of it as painting or whatever else your thing happens to be.

Competition of any kind turns me on tremendously. When I finally left coaching three years ago, I knew I would have difficulties making a transition. I was like the addict going cold turkey. Wow, you go through the horrors when you have honed your life to such a competitive edge. I needed competition like an addict needs his fix.

To this day competition turns me on and makes me completely unreasonable. In tennis I eat up that poor net, man! Oh, Lord, yeah—without the slightest compunction, without the slightest guilt attached to it. And *yet I'm very compassionate by nature. I help little old ladies down the street and that kind of thing. And I react emotionally. I can watch some stupid television show and have tears running down my eyes. Yet, as I say, when the whistle blows that's competition. And competitive drive makes a superstar of any athlete. It raises you a little above the good ones, but even above the great. A guy who can complement physical ability with this kind of mental approach is the guy who stays at the top of the heap a little bit longer, that's all. So it's helpful, if it doesn't carry you to extremes, which we've seen in every level of our society—Watergate, falsifying enrollment records to qualify for government grants, some little kid's father fixing his soap box so he'd win the derby—all in the name of competition, doing it to him before he does it to you.*

In my own experience I became aware of these extremes even coaching and recruiting in college where I was being pushed into gray areas in terms of violating rules—all because of this extreme desire to be successful and win. I saw the killer instinct leading me into excesses, not as a player, because I wasn't even aware of it in those days, but as a coach on the college level. I could see myself going more and more into gray areas and doing things I didn't want to do for the sake of maintaining a success. At that point I decided I could do other things. Now I get as motivated for my little old game of doubles with three old men as I used to for an NBA game, that's all.

To this day, if I could become the Howard Hughes of the sports world, I would. I like people individually, but not in large numbers at all. I never liked the spotlight. I don't function well in that kind of atmosphere. I was always very realistic in terms of my talent. I was always appropriately humble. Affection of any kind has always upset me because of my early shyness and being something of an introvert. I like to have people say, "That's so-and-so," but the bottom line is simply that I prefer my privacy more and more. It's much easier for me to give up the exposure than it would be for me to go and seek it.

I think that's what it's all about. If you don't need to keep following that bouncing ball, you should stop and do whatever is important to you. Unfortunately, many people keep chasing that ball until they die, and in that whole time have never stopped to enjoy whatever they could enjoy out of the rest of life.

Bill Sharman

They didn't have basketball on the West Coast until about 1958 or 1959, so as I was growing up, baseball was the glamor sport. I wasn't interested in basketball. My big ambition and desire was to be a major league baseball player.

I signed a bonus contract to play in the major leagues when I went to USC. If you signed such a contract at that time, you had to go to the majors. Finally, I signed with the Brooklyn Dodgers, but I figured it would take me three or four years to get established, so I played pro basketball on the side. I had played both in college, but baseball was what I wanted to make it in. The competition, the financial aspects—it was my sport. The Dodgers had a really good team then—Duke Snider, Carl Furillo, Jackie Robinson—and what happened? It turned out I moved up faster in basketball. After four years of doing both I had to make a decision between the two. Today, I look at baseball and it almost bores me it seems so slow.

I go far enough back to where we pioneered the league. Then there were two or three leagues, the traveling was tough, and we didn't get paid very much money. Those pressures were different from the ones today. My first year with the Celtics we only played sixty-two games compared to the eighty-two played today. The game was different then, too. Today there is more stress on the body because there's more running. It's a faster game. All the teams fast-break and run now, unlike before, so the players have to be in better shape. Also, the longer season means more games, still more running. When I played, the game was rougher; there was more pushing and shoving and more fights. We always had two or three players who the coach—Red Auerbach—used for testing other players. At that time the rules were that if a fight broke out between two players, both got thrown out. So coaches would hire a twelfth man to pick on a Cousy or a Bill Russell.

Since there were fewer teams, there were fewer jobs, and the traveling was rougher. Although we traveled mostly by plane or train, my first year coach, Bones McKinney, was afraid to fly, so we didn't take one airplane trip the entire season. It often took two and a half days just to get to one game. One time we dressed in a taxi and still got there thirty minutes late.

Today the players have to be in a little better shape. Next to boxers I think basketball players have to be in the best shape. You have to have endurance and quickness and you have to sustain the running. You're running back and forth and then you have to make an all-out effort to jump like a high jumper. Sometimes you've got to go up three or four times. If you're not in great shape, it shows. Your legs get wobbly, the ball feels like it's coming out of your hands, and you feel the stress in your stomach. It just takes everything out of you. You have to be conditioned like both a sprinter and a distance runner.

To be a great player or to have a great team you have to have what we call contact and muscle. It's a very, very physical game. You've also got to have great body balance; otherwise you get faked out of position. You might be the greatest shooter in the world, but if that defense man's got his hand in your face, you won't get that shot off.

I think basketball's such a beautiful finesse game, almost like a ballet. Put Bill Russell—when he used to go up he had a little flick of the hand— or a Julius Erving on film and slow it down. God, it's beautiful!

I've always enjoyed sports. They've always been important to me. I think there are a lot of reasons why we do things. For me, being in good shape is important and I like to compete; it's fun and challenging. And of all the sports I've played, basketball was the most fun in all respects. I was thirty-five my last year and I was in good shape because I worked at it. I always enjoyed the practices as well as playing. But those last three or four years I knew I was coming to an end. I used to sustain more injuries and it took longer for them to heal. If we played three or four games in a row, I didn't bounce back as quickly those last nights. So I thought about being a coach. I started keeping notebooks on different plays and situations that would arise during a game. Basketball is just so much a part of my life. I always want to be associated with it and with the people. I can go to almost any city and I have three or so pretty good friends there. The friends you make are a very valuable part of pro ball.

It's very complicated being a coach. You're functioning as an executive, a coordinator, a secretary—but mostly you're dealing with personalities. Having been a player, I think, helped me. The team is more respectful, knowing I've been through it. It's harder for a coach who hasn't played to push his team. You practice three times a day in preseason. You really torture the players. You have to. I remember as a player how I ached—my stomach, my legs, my feet.

Today the players are stronger and better than we were, but it seems 90 percent of them have to be pushed. Maybe 5 or 10 percent will work on their own without somebody telling them to. I'm not a good judge of this because I played with a super team. But it didn't seem as though we had to be pushed by Red Auerbach like we're pushing our players today. I'm a little bit surprised and disappointed in some players. With all the financial gain, publicity, and personal pride these players could achieve by being really dedicated, it seems that more of them would push themselves. It's very frustrating as a coach. I've seen so many players who had the ability to be superstars, but they just wouldn't make themselves do it. It's been a mystery to me, what with all that's at stake today. Maybe there are too many distractions. In my day we didn't make the high salaries; we didn't have the investments, the meetings with lawyers, or the same social life. Sometimes I think the desire in a person, how competitive he is, might be an innate quality. It might be something a kid is born with. It's not a disgrace to lose, but it is downgrading. It might be that some kids are afraid of putting themselves in a position to lose. It's really a mystery to me why they don't push harder!

There's a lot of pressure in the game, too. You know you're putting on a performance for people. I would think in a way that comes under the heading "art." We use the words performance, show business, great feats—but I don't hear the word art very much. I have to say that to give a great performance, to play a great game—that's art. An athlete has to get himself up for a game; he has to get inside himself and excite himself.

Other performers have pressure also, but the winning or losing aspect isn't there. You work harder for every game and every different situation to react, respond, fake, and maneuver. There's pressure in just working yourself up to that every game. Then if you lose, you just feel lousy, even though you may have played a good game. You also know you're not going to get much sympathy—not from the press or the fans. All you're going to hear is "You got beat," and that's a very uncomfortable feeling.

As a coach you feel creative in a different way. You don't respond and react individually, but you try to organize the plays, the patterns, the practice sessions. There's a different kind of gratification. One of the toughest parts for me as a coach was sitting on the bench. I wanted to go out there and be active. I'm a doer, a physical person, and I hated just sitting there. I missed the competition a tremendous amount also. As I said, I guess that's born in some people. I don't really know why. I'd probably be happier if I didn't have that feeling, because when you compete, you've got to go through the losing process and I hate to lose. But the feeling is there and I guess I'll always be that way.

Naturally, I don't regret anything. I've been very lucky. I've been able to fulfill all my goals and dreams in sports. I haven't thought about my next dream or goal for a while. Basketball has been very good to me; it's been the number one thing in my life next to my family and my religion. I certainly have no complaints. I'm very fortunate, considering I always thought I wanted to be a baseball player.

Bob Pettit

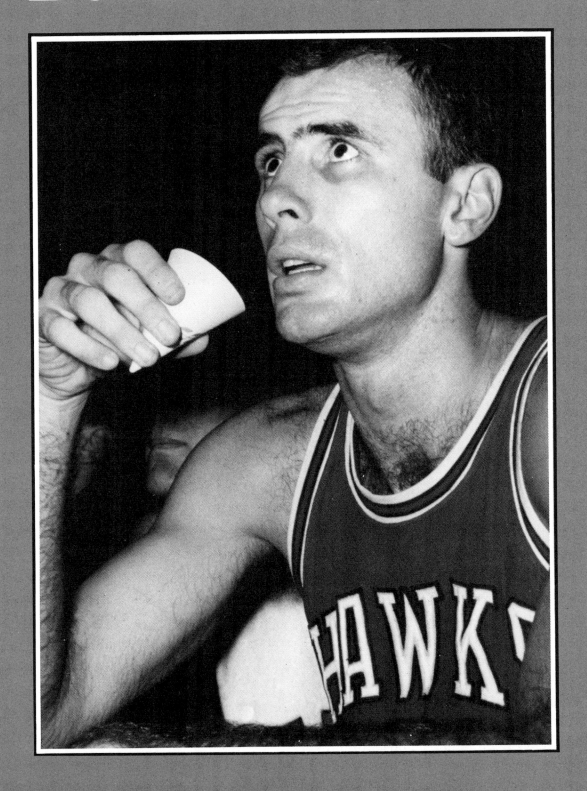

When I was a freshman in high school I went out for everything—football, baseball, basketball, and track. I think I was like most boys in those days. I just wanted to participate in athletics. As a freshman my ambition was just to letter by the time I was a senior. If you made a team, you got a jacket with the initials of the school on it. I didn't make it at all. I was cut from the basketball team. I was very uncoordinated, very tall, 5 feet 9 and weighed 118 or 120 pounds, and I went out for all these sports which basically I wasn't good enough to play. My parents encouraged me to continue and they set up a goal in the backyard. I used to practice every afternoon after school. I had lights set up at night and I'd go out and shoot. I worked awfully hard. I was not content not to play. I really don't know why; it just seemed the thing to do. So I just continued working on it.

As a sophomore I started playing in a YMCA league and started to develop a bit. I was still awfully thin, but I did continue to grow and develop coordination. I used to jump rope and lift weights. I just continued to practice, and the coordination came and there I was. Actually, when I look back on it, one of the best things that ever happened was that I was not so good to start with, so I had to work so much harder to get where I was going. I went out for basketball again as a junior. I'd grown to about 6 feet 5 and weighed 150 or 155 pounds. I did well as a junior, made the all-city team in Baton Rouge and went to the state tournament. I didn't do too well there. But I came back as a senior in high school and had a very good year.

The thing I remember the most from my college years was how bad I was to start with. What amazed my friends in later years was the fact that the people who knew me then never dreamed that I could play high school basketball, much less college basketball. It was an awful lot of hard work, time, and effort. I had mumps in my senior year in high school and I sat out nine games. Then I came back and we won fifteen or seventeen games in a row, including the state championship. I started to play extremely well, probably averaging 20 points a game. I really progressed. Then by my freshman year in college I had grown to about 6 feet 9 and averaged 23 points a game. This was the period of my greatest development as far as skills and working on shots and the different things that went with those. It's probably a common story with basketball players. You just had to go into your backyard and shoot all afternoon, do your lessons, and go back out at night and shoot some more. I can't remember specifically, but it was very natural. Like everybody else, I dreamed of playing in the finals of a national championship or something. Playing basketball was something I enjoyed doing and I developed.

In those days, in my part of the country, we didn't know anything about professional basketball. There was no TV. Probably the only team anybody ever heard of was the Minneapolis Lakers because of George Mikan. I had a distant relative who played basketball with Fort Wayne. He was very close to the family and he had gone to LSU, so I followed his career. They were probably the only two players that I had ever heard of and remembered. Even in college I never thought of being a professional basketball player until my senior year. That was 1954 and I was torn between playing AAU ball and pro ball. Many of the Olympic teams came from the AAU teams, which you'd play for and then have a career with a company like Phillips Petroleum after it was over. But first you'd have an opportunity to play in the Olympics. The pay was not that much different from pro ball.

The only reason I chose pro basketball was that I would have about five months off and could come back to Baton Rouge and work and live there. If I had gone with the AAU company I would not have had the opportunity to return to Louisiana. So that was what made me choose to be a professional basketball player. I was definitely going to play, but where? I wanted to have time off to live in my home town and work there.

When I graduated from college I was the number one choice of the Milwaukee Hawks. My first coach was Red Holzman. He coached the Hawks for about two and a half years. Immediately he moved me from center where I had played in college to the forward position. I think that was the biggest transition I made. It opened up a whole new world for me. I was able to move; I could shoot from outside. The other thing was *that I learned to play defense as a forward. My first year my defense was atrocious. The great thing I had going for me was that we had a very bad team that year. As a rookie I played every minute of every game. They can tell you all they want about how good it is to watch and observe and learn, but there's nothing like playing. If I'd gone with a good team like the Minneapolis Lakers, I'd have been sitting on the bench for a couple of years, watching. Instead, I played forty-eight minutes. I might miss ten shots in a row and make ten mistakes on defense but I still played. It was great and I took very naturally to the forward position. I loved it.*

The main problem was that I had a tough time with the physical pounding you took under the backboard—fighting for the rebound and things. So after my second year I went on a strong weight-lifting program. They had a trainer in Baton Rouge who worked with all the athletes. We used to work out at his health gym. The strongest athletes—when they have the other abilities too—are usually the best. Strength is such an important part of it, not only to take the pounding on the court, but also to be able to take the life you lead as a pro basketball player. Playing five nights a week, every night in a different town, spending your life in trains, buses, and airplanes—it's a very demanding life and it's important that you be strong. I always had to overcome the fact that I was thin. So for the next four or five years I worked hard and built myself up to 240 pounds. I had the shots and moves and naturally learned more in this area, but the biggest gain I made was getting much stronger. I think that psychologically, when you exercise with weights, you get to think you're stronger whether you are or not. You get to the point where you think you're the strongest person out there. I used to work with these heavy punching bags, using the elbows on them, pushing up, lifting weights, isometrics, all these things, and I got to think I was strong. I got to the point where I really loved the pushing and shoving.

I prepared. I can honestly say that I never walked out on a basketball court when I was not as ready as I could possibly be at that moment of play. I psyched myself up every night. I'd do little things. I might be playing in some little town and I'd pick somebody to play to. Or I'd start thinking about the game that afternoon. Who was I going to play? Who was going to play me? What did I need to do that night against that particular defensive player on the opposite team? Then I'd walk out on the court. Being single, I'd pick out some good-looking girl in the audience and say to myself, I'm going to play to her. Or I might have a relative there. Or it might be in New York. You never really needed to psych yourself up there. If it was a night in Detroit in the Olympia and maybe it was on top of ice and fifty or sixty degrees in the place with three hundred or a thousand people, that was the night you really had to do what I'm talking about. That doesn't mean that on some nights I wouldn't be more ready to play than on other nights, but I was really able to get myself up to play. I never needed a coach to prepare me. It was pride. Maybe that's what it was. I really don't know.

There's no question that as a player you're an entertainer. I always wanted people to go away and feel that they had gotten their money's worth. I was very conscious of the fans. Maybe one or two came to see me play. Everything I did was geared to those two hours. I took care of myself as far as how late I stayed out at night before a game and what I ate. I was always very conscious of these things. I was ready to play basketball every night. Basketball was a foundation for me. It was a way for me to advance myself toward a business career when I finished playing.

I worked every off-season with my family in the real estate business. I had always planned to go into the business. Being an only child, my parents talked a lot around me about the business. My mother was a very good businesswoman. I hadn't thought about it until now, but that probably oriented me in that direction because real estate was the thrust of our family conversation.

In those days of pro ball there was not that much money involved. As a rookie in 1954 I made $11,000. I might take that amount I made and save $6,000 of it. I came back to Baton Rouge and invested it. I bought two small family houses my first year. I don't want to give the impression that I played strictly for money. I would have done it for very little because I did love it. But I was very fortunate to realize that being an athlete was a very short-lived existence. There comes a day when all of a sudden you're no longer the king of the mountain and you have to go out and

work like everybody else. I felt that athletics was a small part of my life. It was something that I loved very much, something that I would have done for nothing, but I realized that one day I would be thirty-two years old. So I went to work. I think the best thing I did was try to prepare myself for the time when I no longer was going to play.

I had an opportunity very few people ever have. I was very successful in my profession. It was an opportunity that lots of people think about but very few people achieve. It was not tough on me to travel. I was single. It was very exciting. I would enjoy being in New York, Los Angeles, San Francisco. I had no ties to hold me. I would rather be there than in my apartment in St. Louis. But I felt that I never wanted to play when I *couldn't play to the standards that I set for myself. In my ninth year I was twenty-nine, thirty. I could feel that I was not the player that I was at twenty-seven or twenty-eight. I was a lot smarter, but I could feel that I wasn't really as strong, that I couldn't jump as high as I once did. So I notified my owner that I was quitting in two years. I was ready to get away from it and I did it, knowing that one of the deadest things in the world is to see an old athlete—an athlete who can't divorce himself from his memories and realize he's no longer an athlete.*

I've always been lucky. I've always had people interested in me—like the chairman of the board of this bank I went to work for in Baton Rouge. I quit playing in April 1965. I got married. I had other things that interested me more than basketball. As a former athlete I had an advantage. In the banking business, like athletics, you're selling yourself; you're selling your bank. It was a plus being Bob Pettit. People at the bank say, "Oh, they love to talk to you." Usually they remember when you played. But that's all it does. You've got to be able to convince them that you can handle their business better than the bank they're currently dealing with. You're not going to sell a guy because you're old Joe Blow. All things are equal, but as a former athlete you do have an advantage.

I don't know if I outgrew the game. I think the key was that I really had something to go to that I could look forward to. But it's awfully difficult to make the transition. I completely divorced myself from basketball. I think subconsciously I'd seen so many athletes who weren't able to face retirement. I just didn't want to be in that position. I can look back and remember when I was playing: The locker room door would open and in would come some guy who had played five years ago and you would say, "Oh, here comes that guy again." I just closed that door. I really went too far, but I love what I'm doing. I've become very involved in the community. The bank is doing extremely well. Now I go to see a few games and I enjoy it. As I said earlier, at thirteen my ambition was to be better by the time I was a senior. I can remember that was a definite goal, one I worked toward. Earlier than that I just don't remember anything. You set goals for yourself in your life and your career. I have been very lucky and things look awfully good for me now.

Oscar Robertson

My mother worked as a domestic. One day she got a basketball for me and brought it home. From that day on I started bouncing the ball around the house until I got sense enough to go outside and shoot at an actual hoop. In the background I came from, you didn't have money to do other things. Where I lived everybody was poor, so naturally I turned to sports. It was something to do to pass the time away, to get together, to meet socially. I played all sports, but my brother started to play basketball before I entered high school. He went to an all-black school in Indianapolis, where our team was successful. I naturally followed him.

We played football and baseball in the middle of the day and basketball, usually, when the sun went down. So we were playing some kind of ball all day long. I kept my basketball with me all the time. I was always teased about it—about dribbling balls all over the neighborhood. I carried my basketball like a musician carries his trumpet with him all the time. It was true love! I loved to play but I actually never thought of playing pro till I got to college. I was at school in Cincinnati. They had a team and I got to play on it. I saw the Globetrotters play a few times when I was in high school, so this was my only connection with pro ball. I went to college on a basketball scholarship even though my grades were very good in high school.

Playing was not a dream per se. It was the competition I was thinking about—whether I could actually compete and on what level. I practiced all the time by myself. People thought I was really out of it, but there was something about it I didn't mind. I thought I could play. I don't know if I can say that I was obsessed with playing, but it kind of took over. I believe with some people, especially athletes, you have to compete. Early on I played a game against some team, I don't remember which team right now, and scored in the teens, the low teens. I heard the comment, "Oh, Oscar is not that great a player. He was real easy tonight." I said to myself, well, buddy, we'll go around again. The next time it was a little bit different; I scored quite a few points against them. A small thing like that, a little comment, whether he meant it or not, really spurred me on.

You don't want anyone to embarrass you on the court. Everybody, no matter who he is or what he says, thinks he's a certain kind of player. I felt I could play just about anybody because basketball was all I did, so I didn't want anybody to take away what I really thought about myself deep inside. My coach told me something in high school and it's always been with me. He said, "Once you play sports, you're always going to have your ups and downs, but one thing is for sure. No matter what anyone says about you, you're the one who has to play." You hope to go out and do something good. I may not like what the person has said, but that does not take away from my ability on the court or how well I play basketball. That's up to me. This is the idea I've always kept with me.

I try to focus on my own inner life. When you play you're out there; you've got to watch what the guys are doing. They'll steal the ball from you or they'll score on you so you have to be on guard. My primary function in the pros was to control the game setup: find out who was scoring, who was scoring from what position on the court, know when to run and when to slow the ball down, break the momentum and pick it up—all these things. You've got to watch and concentrate every minute. Like in baseball, you've got to watch the hands from the time the pitcher looks to get the signal from the catcher. You've always got to be ready. Basketball's the same. It's a mental discipline. You have to know the things fundamentally; play the game whether dribbling, shooting, guarding. You have to be so intent that you don't let anything else into your thoughts. Like a dancer, you've rehearsed so many times you don't go out and worry about making mistakes or about all the things outside. You've got to maintain your equilibrium at all times. Things are going to be real upsetting as you go through life, so you've got to maintain a certain quality and serenity about a lot of situations. You're confident. You go right on; you go through the routine. This is the way it was with me.

You've got to be able to say, "No one can do the things that I can do with a basketball. I can play with anybody." You've always got to have this. You can't go out in any contest and say, "I don't know if I can do it. This guy, maybe he'll beat us, or maybe I can't do this with this team." I didn't think that anybody could outplay me on the court. Nobody.

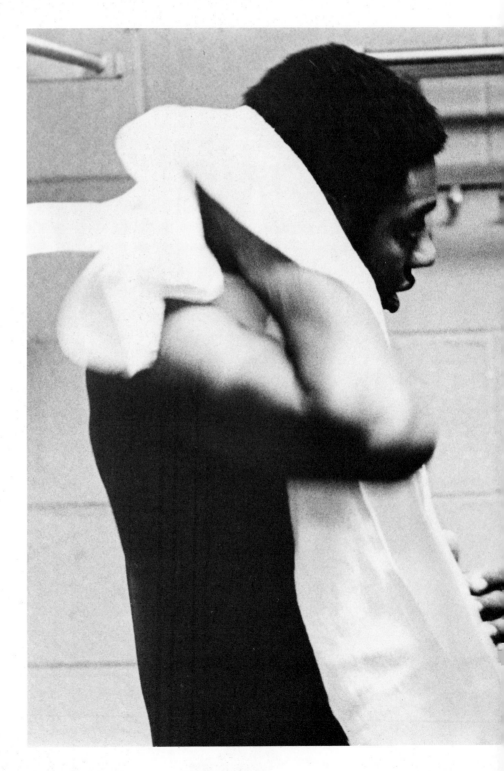

I really enjoyed playing. It was a special thing for me, and the guys were my friends always. It's very artistic. If someone would take a slow motion camera and watch some guy make his moves, show all the different angles—the leg kicks, the pushing and shoving, jumping, rebounding, stretching your arms—you might see a few pirouettes. It's very artistic indeed.

I haven't stopped totally. It's a little different now. I miss the competition, some of the people I worked with. I never understand why people make such a big do about playing ball or not. It's just something I did. Maybe I'm not as much out of it as other people are. I simply enjoy playing. Whatever I had I was happy for and I'm happy I played the way I did. My good times were when I played. I like to meet people; I'm a people person. I like to travel and meet people all over the world. I have a lot of new visions. This is what basketball gave to me.

I'll tell you something. When I was seven or eight years old, where was I? What dreams could I have? People who lived where I did didn't have dreams about anything. They were just living, drifting. To have dreams you have to have your curiosity aroused, to see different things, talk to people about things, read books. I loved to do this. That's how I got into basketball, and that's when I started to dream about something else. I used to look up at airplanes and wonder where in the world they were going. And I'd dream about the people in business. What would it be like for me to be in charge of something everybody needs. But at that early age I didn't have anything to dream about. I never had anything to miss.

When you live in a ghetto, man, you've got to fight. It's a way of life. My only dream was getting out, going to school, keep from getting beat up. That was the dream I had then.

Jerry West

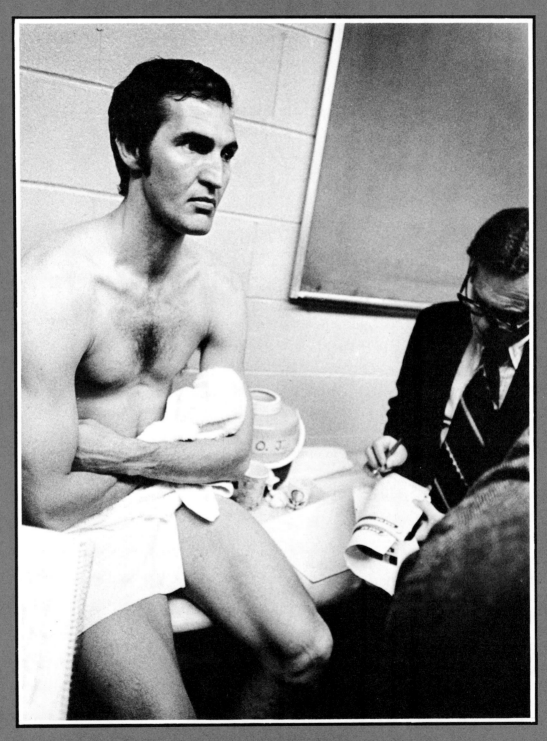

When I played I didn't realize what I was doing was very important. It was something I really enjoyed, like a kid playing a game. So I really didn't place much importance on it. To be honest, I really never thought I was very good. I always looked at the negative things about my playing, and if we got beaten, it was my fault. I really think a lot of it is a reflection of the fact that when I was little I used to be able to beat anyone.

The key word is play. In a place like West Virginia there wasn't very much to do except sports. There were a number of kids who played basketball and some of them were pretty good. Just watching, I developed an interest, but I really think the fact that I had so much spare time and that there wasn't a lot to do, I sort of gravitated towards basketball. I can remember when I couldn't shoot the ball up to the basket overhand, so I had to shoot underhand. That's the way it started.

I think one of the great fascinations basketball had, particularly to kids from small towns, was that your mind was a tremendous motivator. I mean, you could play five guys—have four teammates in your mind. I can remember games where the team in my own mind scored 100 points and I scored 89 of them, or 98, and I let one guy score 1 basket. You could make the winning shot and they carried you off the floor. The mind allows you tremendous flexibility.

As I got a little older I had the desire to play on some level. First I wanted to play on the junior high school level in seventh grade, but I couldn't make the team. By the ninth grade I made the team but I wasn't very good. I was small and not growing very much. Then in high school I played on the junior varsity team, but I was still very small. All of a sudden one summer I grew, I think, almost to 6 feet 2. I was very awkward and weak. It seemed like I was always tired, yet I had a tremendous desire to play. Summer and winter, when there was snow on the ground, I played all the time, constantly. It was something I really loved. Then I sort of woke up one day and I was better. It was my junior year and my senior year I developed even more. Then there were numerous scholarship offers, but I went to a school where no one bought me because I wanted to go there—my state university.

I am thirty-nine now and it seems very strange to say that at that time pro basketball was a young sport, but it was. I didn't have anyone I idolized because there was no TV nor a lot of media coverage. Now with that exposure and publicity, kids tend to pick a player. They can be a Jerry West, a Kareem Abdul Jabbar, a Julius Erving—some player who they can say in their mind, hey, I can be like that. That's tremendous for kids, plus the fact that you can play basketball with one ball, one basket, and you don't need anyone around in order to learn.

I think maybe the biggest disappointment early in an athlete's life is that you get to a certain point and all of a sudden you're beaten. When you played that imagined foe by yourself you never quit because you knew you were going to win. You'd beaten him from the time you were eight years old, and when you've beaten that guy all your life and now you start to play competitively and you're beaten, you can't understand it. I had self-doubt because we lost against teams that I couldn't believe we could lose to. It weighed heavily. All the times we played in the play-offs and came so close so many times to winning, yet we couldn't, I'd say, "Are we jinxed? Do we choke?" I'd analyze myself and say, you've done this; you've accomplished that. And you find out it's not what you do as an individual, but what you do as a team. Our team had success. We got there every year, but we didn't have it in the championships.

I think it gets back to the self-motivating thing in the sense that you push yourself and you achieve on the individual level and on the team level. The individual level really doesn't matter so much, except for the respect of your peers. Pushing your will, your basketball personality, on the other people around you, you're completely ad-libbing. I'd see something a team was doing and say, "Hey, as soon as I get the ball, you just take off." And I'd turn around and didn't even have to look, because I knew the guy would be there. I think about four years in my career I averaged 30 points a game, and there were lots of nights I knew I could score up in the 50s. Yet that's just not the way to do it. It's a self-defeating thing when you talk about scoring a lot of points, because you have to learn to play with the other team members. Every once in a while you come upon teams where personalities mesh. They are exceptionally

gifted mentally; they know how to play the game the way it should be played, and you'll see these teams do incredible things. Then again, I've played where we were just cast in our own separate molds. You have to score more points for that team to be successful—you're forcing your basketball personality on the floor that night. It's a nice feeling to know that you can do that some nights, but if it's not for the right reasons, then it's self-defeating and it destroys the chemistry of the team.

Athletes are very normal when they first start out. Then all of a sudden their egos get involved and they change. If someone writes something derogatory about them, my goodness! They can't believe it. If you give a bad performance you should be criticized, but they never learn to accept that. They're more fragile and living in a glass cage.

I think one of the real tough things about professional basketball is the fact that you have to sustain yourself over eighty-two games and then that part of the season is over. You forget it but then you have to sustain yourself through the playoffs. Some people can never do that; they can perform in one area but not in another. As long as I've played basketball, there are only seven to eight guys who I've considered very special. It's a strange thing when the New York or Los Angeles papers say some guy is a superstar. These people are trying to build you into a great, great basketball player, and I look at them and say, "There is no way that this guy is great." Yet in his mind he suddenly starts to believe he's a super player and because he's not, he can't accept what he can't accomplish.

It's such a fickle kind of a world. When everything goes right, everything looks rosy. But very early I realized that when things go wrong, the same people who would say something nice then say to someone else, "The guy's terrible." You're still the same person no matter what.

That's why athletes like kids. A kid isn't so prejudiced in his judgment; adults are less objective. The respect of all the kids in the country who say this guy is the best player in that position that there is—that's the thing that appeals to you. I really like people very much, but if they would sort of be consistent with their feelings towards you, I think it would be a lot easier to accept your role.

Was I ever aware of my stature as a player? I think you only develop that from the time you start playing, when you develop the confidence that you are becoming better. I honestly never paid much attention to myself. I didn't realize some of the things I'd accomplished as a player. I just had a tremendous drive to sell and to win. I wanted to be the best, and the only way you can try to be the best is when you're not very good. It makes you drive every night, play harder every night. Then suddenly you get to the point and say, I am superior to those other people. If you feel that way, then the nicest feeling in the world is to go out on that floor knowing you're better than every one of those players. That's a tremendous advantage.

The most mentally taxing thing for a player is when you're hurt and you have to go out there and play. It doesn't take very long to lose the edge that you have as an athlete, and it's frustrating when you go out there and you know you're really physically not ready to play.

I think I could contribute the last two years of my career, because I was playing with good players. But the self-doubt sort of starts to creep in if you lose the ability to attack. You go up to shoot and your legs are not quite strong enough to hold you there. Some nights you're strong, some you're not. It's not like being twenty-eight, thirty, where you're physically better than everyone. Then at thirty-one, thirty-two, you start to have nights when your legs are not so good. A crucial play that you could have made if you were physically strong, you don't make. Players have to accept the responsibility that they're going to lose this agility, and that's when the huge egos start to crumble. Later in my career I was physically just not able to contribute.

I didn't agonize over it. It was time for me to stop playing. I knew that day would come.

The thing I missed about basketball was the way of life. You know, I never worked, basically, from the time I went to college. And if you have someone good working for you, after a few years as a pro player your future is really pretty good from a financial aspect. So probably the pressure that I imposed on myself was something that was just nice to get away from. I'd been told to go to school at a certain time, catch an air-

plane at this time, eat at this time, practice at this time. And suddenly I said, this is the greatest not to have to do that. But then you get away and you say, I miss going to practice a little—the kidding with the guys, a nap before the game, eating at a certain time. The mental preparation of getting ready to play and doing that for so many years becomes ingrained. But playing for the crowd response, for the fame, I didn't miss that, no sir!

It's a tremendously wearing thing to go out there every night and just work and work and work till you don't have anything physically left to give. And when you're doing that against the worst team and the best team, then you just say, my God. Enough's enough. I can remember nights late in my career. I'm sitting in my locker room, my head down before the ball game, saying there's no way I can play this game. I'm sore. I felt like a racehorse every damn minute. Emotionally I can't make myself play. Then you go out there, and you start shooting lay-ups. Your legs hurt. I remember a lot of games after eight minutes in the first quarter I suddenly started to get loose, and I felt maybe I could play a little bit. And then you had to play three nights in a row, which we had to do frequently. I'd get to the point where I just didn't know if I could. You're so into the inner drive I guess private performance, individual pride—those are the things that make you do it.

I played basketball fourteen years professionally, through the formative years of my life while other people were out trying to establish what they were going to do later. I always thought, maybe I'll go back to school and do something constructive, but I think when you become financially secure you really become independent and then you don't care much. It's not easy for me to sit around mentally idle. I couldn't stand myself. That's basically what it got to and there was nothing else I knew.

Coaching is a tremendous learning process. I would say coaches who have less talent have a chance to be better than those who have more talent. The more talented people do not want to be structured, restricted. To coach you have to have been analytical about the game. It also helps to have the ability to communicate.

I feel in trying to be successful it's how much you want to work at it. Physically you have to be strong, but the most important part of it is the mental aspect.

Everyone has something different they want to do. Some people have an offense that's structured to do this kind of shot, others are restricted to create a shot that's close to the basket. There are all kinds of ways to win. The creative part is sort of restricted with basketball. The thing that every coach likes is movement. If you can't get correct movement and don't have quick people who can think, you're not going to win. If they are gifted and you can get your players to believe they can win in any way, I would say that's creative.

As a coach the elation is not the same as for a player. Physically, you don't have much control over what's going on out there. You find that you don't sleep; you worry more. The elation is not the same when you win. It's a great feeling to go out there and play hard. You come in, take a shower, collect your thoughts and it's done. As a coach, you go back, make notes—can we physically do something? Are they going to be good? What to do in practice? As a player you've been trained, conditioned. You do things instinctively. As a coach it doesn't look that way.

It's a big responsibility. You can't satisfy everyone, but I know that I'm just out to try to communicate with these guys and to make them happy. If they're not happy they're not going to have fun, and if they don't have any fun, they're not going to win. It's a game you should have fun with. If you don't. . . forget it.

John Havlicek

My career has seen many cycles. I was the youth of the Celtics from 1962 until 1969, and then I became the old man in one year because of all the retirements. We struggled for a few years before winning the championship in 1974 and 1976. So I've been part of two generations. I don't know of many people who have gone through that big a cycle. I've been old for seven or eight years now. That label doesn't really bother me. I know I'm not going to play forty-eight minutes of every ball game. I know I'm going to play between twenty-five and thirty-two, something like that. I realize that the owners of the team and most knowledgeable people know I can't do what I once used to. But during those twenty-five or thirty minutes, or whatever I play, I feel that I do contribute as much and probably more than somebody else could contribute in my role.

I'm coming off the bench again. There's no one who's been able to do that since Silas left. We've tried different people but no one could assume that role with any consistency, so it's given me another lift. The coach is happy about it and I feel that my playing has been unusual because I play both forward and guard. I've come off the bench and I've been a server. I like the feeling of being versatile. I'm not what I used to be, but I still contribute a great deal. It is frustrating at times, but then again I have to be realistic and level with myself a little bit. There are things I just can't achieve any more. You must do what you can within the realm of possibility rather than stargaze about the past.

Probably the biggest thing for me to accept, along with Don Nelson, who came in the same year I did and Paul Silas, who is no longer with the team, is that the camaraderie I grew up with is now gone. I'm more or less a throwback from the older generation when the NBA was struggling and it was difficult sometimes to get enough meal money and that type of thing. So there are times when I say to myself, "What am I doing here?" Then I look at myself and say, "What else can I do as well, and what else would I enjoy as much?" Then right away I'm back into it. I still have a good feeling for the game and I'm not tired of it or anything. I don't think I'd enjoy working in any other profession as much as I do this one, so I'll continue with it till I can't do it anymore.

I grew up in a very small town in Ohio. Basically, the people who lived in that area were immigrants—coal miners and steel mill workers in the Ohio Valley. Really the only outlet that people had was sports—football, baseball, basketball, hunting, and fishing. I can remember bouncing and shooting a basketball when I was five years old. I have an older brother and a sister. I was the tagalong. My brother didn't want me around, but I proved myself in a lot of respects. When they played some sport I filled out the team and I remember even as a youngster I was generally better than most of the people my own age. When we played basketball, if there were three people, it would be two on one or one on two, and I was always the one. It was even that way in football when the older kids were playing. If they needed another person to play with, they'd sort of look around the playground and then choose me because I was the best of what was left of the younger lot. So invariably I always got taken. I happened to have a little more ability and that gave me a feeling of pride.

I never concentrated on any sport. I played all of them in high school. Then when I went to college I decided that I wanted to play basketball because that's the one I liked the most. I felt that if you had a smaller group—there are five in basketball, nine in baseball, and eleven in football—you'd be a little closer. I've always enjoyed the relationship of being with a team and seeing it develop to a point where you can depend on one another, when you can complement another person to help him become a better player. I think this is one of the biggest tributes you can pay a person.

When I got to college I really started to play on a very high level. We won the national championship. I don't think we could have achieved that without a certain amount of respect for each other in the way we played the game. We were five people working as a unit.

I had no idea of how good I really was because when I went to Ohio State most of the write-ups were about Jerry Lucas. Larry Siegfried had the state scoring record the year before. He was one year older than we were. Mel Nowell and Joe Roberts were both from Columbus, Ohio, so I was like the black sheep from the small town way down in the hills, a where-did-he-come-from? type person. But I was happy to be there and started to realize that I must have been quite a decent player to make the team.

As the years passed I realized that there were people paying attention to me in regard to my ability. I can remember my freshman class at Ohio State. If you put all the scoring averages together it would have averaged over 150 points a game. The coach was selling defense. Even though I had been a great scorer in high school, I wanted to play, so I just more or less abandoned my offense and became so involved defensively that I was able to make the team. I guess people were watching and seeing how hard I worked, and because of the unit we had they started to work just as hard defensively. I think that any time you have success, in basketball in particular, it's because of the defense. So I feel lucky to have had that distinction of being the defensive man in college.

John Havlicek

I had been very close to my high school coaches and sort of looked on myself as being somewhat like them. During the season we would have a certain relationship, while during the off days in the summer we were always involved in a lot of camping trips, fishing trips to Canada, and that type of thing. I really liked that kind of life. I figured I would go to school and play ball, become a coach, and more or less follow along those lines. It wasn't until the latter part of my junior and senior years in college that I realized there were other things I could be interested in—namely, being a professional athlete. There were all kinds of scouts from various pro organizations there. And even being invited to the Olympic trials one year indicated that I might have some ability, because they didn't take just anyone at that particular time. I felt there was a chance, but I wasn't basing my whole life on it because if I didn't make it I was prepared to become a coach. I didn't want any big letdown or disappointment.

When I graduated from Ohio State I went into pro football. At that time I looked at the money situation. Salaries were the same, but the schedule was not in favor of basketball. You played eighty-some games as opposed to fourteen in football. I was from Ohio and was drafted by the Cleveland Browns. That was my favorite football team. For me to make an adjustment, pick up my roots, and start in another place would have been a hassle. It was much easier for me to decide on football.

Even though I hadn't played since high school, I said to myself, if I don't make it, the good Lord is trying to tell me something. So I gave it one shot and that was it. I was with the Browns for about six weeks and played in a couple of exhibition games. I was the last receiver cut by the team, so I knew that I did have some ability. But there were a lot of veterans on the team. I knew it was a very good team and I had come close to making it. So in June I graduated from college, went to football training camp in July, got cut in August, and started basketball in September.

Everything then sort of fell in line. It was easy for me. One of the things that I'm proudest of now is that I played in more NBA games than any other player. You can look at all my accomplishments in scoring and all the championship teams and games I've been part of, but playing that many games has to rank really high up there because no one has done it before. It's a nice feeling.

I've always tried to do certain things. Throughout my basketball career there has always been room for improvement, and I believe you improve to different plateaus. The first year I was just happy to get off the bench and contribute. My motivation was to keep on pushing so that I wouldn't have any setbacks. My second year I led the team in scoring, which was something I didn't exactly strive for—it seemed to come naturally. So I've always had this thing in my mind—to strive for a level of consistent excellence within whatever plateau I was on. Now, an injury or something like that can set you back. But if there's no real reason to have a setback, if you're physically and emotionally well, then you must strive to maintain that level of consistency.

Over the years you improve to a peak; probably between the ages of twenty-eight and thirty-two you're at your highest level. You know when you reach your peak. Now my level is starting to decline a little because of the age factor and because we have a lot of younger players who are able to do a lot of the things that I did when I was younger. It's hard sometimes to accept that you're not doing as much. But then again, when you look at the overall team structure you really are contributing. Maybe not statistically, but emotionally and mentally. Like when I'm playing a game, one of the things I remind myself is—and it's probably what has contributed to my stamina, my endurance—that it becomes a mental game after a while. When you have been playing thirty or forty minutes you look at the other person and he looks like he's a little tired. Maybe you feel a little tired too, and you say to yourself, who's going to wear down first? Mentally you keep pushing yourself so that you don't give in to that game and lose the mental battle. This is probably where I developed endurance. I did this at a very young age in high school. I would see a person get tired and I'd realize, man, I got an easy basket, or I made an extra 2 or 3 yards, or I saw a pitcher wearing down in the latter part of the game. I'd take him for that hit, get a good piece of bat on the ball. These are opportunities and perceptions that you have to figure out for yourself.

I really never set any goals for myself. I think they more or less take care of themselves. I don't think you have to be a tough disciplinarian. I sort of like a person who, when he makes a mistake, just buckles down to see that it won't happen again, a person who has a certain toughness about him. If I walk through the house and hit myself or something, I get infuriated with myself. It might hurt like crazy but I won't yell or scream or anything. I just tell myself what a dumb bunny I am for not being careful.

I am hard on myself in a lot of ways, which is what brings out the best in me. I don't know why or how to explain it. But when I was a child, I wasn't allowed to have a bicycle because I lived on a very busy street and my parents didn't want me riding in front of a car. All my friends had bikes and most of the time you went somewhere on your bike. Well, I had to run all the time, so I was always running to keep up with the crew. Within myself I thought of it as having a little toughness—they were getting there easily and I was pushing myself to do it.

When I first started pro ball I thought ten years would be the magic number and I figured if I ever got to the point where I made $25,000, that would be a lot. So there were no fantasies or anything like that. I've been very easygoing all my life. I just sort of blend into the next situation that comes along. I came from a very humble beginning and it's not going to be hard for me to go back to that life-style. I don't feel as though the world will end when basketball ends, because I'll be adjusting to that very easily, I think. But I have had the regimentation and discipline, and I like that because it keeps my mind active. One of the pitfalls a lot of athletes fall into when they get away from this regimentation is that there's so much free time it's really difficult for them to adjust. It's very easy to become lazy if you don't have anything you must do. I think I have enough interests outside basketball that they will keep me going for a while.

What I'll miss the most is the relationship with the people. I've played with them every day, and even though some of the things that go on in the profession are juvenile, the game is the same. And besides, you always grow up keeping some of those kidlike attitudes inside you. Now I meet people my own age in different walks of life and enjoy it. But the strongest ties will always remain with the athletes I've played with.

Elgin Baylor

I never set a goal for my life. I just tried to save money. That's what I was taught as a kid. Other than security and monetary things I thought about a family and kids. No, I didn't set any goals. Even today, I just want to be an average person as far as my life is concerned. I didn't start to do things until I got into pro basketball. I didn't know anyone who had a boat for fishing, for example, so I couldn't go fishing. I became exposed to such things only after I started to play pro basketball. But now I enjoy them. I enjoy being alone. To be honest, I don't enjoy people. I enjoy my own company more. I don't go to a lot of public places because I don't think I can have more fun. When I do things I like to be with close friends, people I enjoy. I don't care what we talk about. If I like them it doesn't matter to me.

When I didn't make the basketball team and I was put in the junior varsity, I thought that was the worst thing that could happen to anybody. When I was a kid, not being able to play in the playground, I thought that was the way it was supposed to be. When I was in high school we had a very good team, undefeated. When they rated the teams the white schools would be first, second, third, fourth, and fifth. They may have lost some games, but we were undefeated and we would be maybe eighth or ninth. How could they judge us when we never played against each other? But when I beat Haynesworth one on one, the guy who had taught me to play, that stayed with me. I never had to prove anything else again. I was satisfied.

So now I just think ahead. Look forward. I don't like to look back. No, I don't. I guess I'm a very private person. I don't care to discuss a lot of things. Some people keep secrets within them for years and years. When they finally share them they still have the secrets, but maybe they feel better. I tend to forget them. I would like to forget them.

Because of my environment it took me until I got into professional basketball to become exposed to a lot of things. I was from a very poor family in Washington, D.C. There was nothing there; the movies were closed to us; segregated. We couldn't go. We had what was supposed to be a public park, but blacks and minorities couldn't play there, so we spent our time entertaining ourselves by playing in the alleys, playing stickball, or maybe *football* if someone was fortunate enough to find a football. We never had a basketball or any place to play with it. When I was fourteen or fifteen it so happened there was a friend of the family, a guy named Clarence Haynesworth, who was at Miami Teacher's College and lived across the street. He played basketball. When he went to play on Saturdays I went with him. Finally they integrated the park playground so we could play there on Saturdays and during the summer when school was out. It was a casual thing. Clarence would work out and I would shoot and play around with him. I had the size, so I enjoyed it. I was maybe 6 feet 2. I had never seen a pro game even though they had the Washington Capitols there. I just couldn't afford to go.

I always loved athletics. I think it was a way of pacifying—satisfying myself. It was an outlet. And I was the type that liked to compete. Because no one else really played basketball, I'd just throw the ball to Clarence and he'd shoot. Eventually we started playing together one on one. Then it got to the point where I wanted to beat him, but I never could for the first two years we played. Finally my goal was to beat him one on one. Then I did and I guess that's what really inspired me to pursue it. I got excited and went out for the boys club and made the team. At that time I was going to high school and I was on the junior varsity team. I went out for the high school team but didn't make it. I was crushed. I thought I was good enough to play with the varsity and I didn't think I would develop or improve my playing while I was with the junior varsity, so I only played a couple of games and quit. I started playing with a recreational league that generally consisted of high school graduates and ex-college players. Competition was so much stronger that it was a way for me to improve. It really worked because I both developed and gained experience. The next year I went out for the varsity team and made it. I was high school all-American.

But even though I was high school all-American I didn't get a lot of athletic scholarships for college. I went to an all-black high school that wasn't canvassed like the white high schools. No one really saw me play. I wanted to get away from Washington, D.C., because I had never been anywhere in my life outside Baltimore and Virginia where my parents

are from. A friend of mine was at a college in Idaho on a football scholarship. He was working there during the summer and the coach asked him if he knew of any other football players, so my friend recommended me. I got a football scholarship to go to college in Idaho. When I got there it rained for two weeks so we never got a chance to go out on the field to practice. We spent two weeks in a gym. Six of the guys on the football team were also on the basketball team so we ended up playing basketball every day. The last day the coach came in and saw me. He was surprised that I could play and said, "I didn't know that you could play basketball." So I said, "You never asked." Then his wheels started turning because he was also the basketball coach, and he asked me if I would be interested in playing basketball instead of football, and I said, "Fine. I'd rather play basketball anyway."

I had never seen a professional basketball game and on Saturdays and Sundays they started showing some of them to us—like the Minneapolis Lakers with George Mikan. I just loved basketball, but in my wildest dreams I never thought of playing pro. One day we were messing with the radio and the NCAA game between University of San Francisco and La Salle University came on. We really got involved in the game and I said, "Gee, it would be great playing in an NCAA championship or for an NCAA school." Then I started thinking it would be nice to go to a bigger school. I wanted to transfer.

After my first year in Idaho we won our conference. Word got out and a couple of schools from the Northwest contacted me about going there. One was Seattle University. It was a big school. They played in the NCAA competition. Since I played in the Northwest I felt people knew more about me there and it would be wiser to stay in the area. So I decided to go to Seattle University for the next three years. I still wasn't thinking of a professional career. I was just a pretty good basketball player. I'd always played. I just took it for granted. I went out there and played because I loved the game and did my job. The only thing I thought about was playing my best and winning. I didn't think beyond that. In my senior year we were in the NCAA competition and we finished second in

the finals. We lost to Kentucky. Then I started thinking pro. After my senior year I was the number one draft pick of the Minneapolis Lakers.

Even though I was the draft choice I was worried about making the team. It thrilled me to be going out there and seeing the guys, because in college you play against some who are intelligent and some who are not, and the competition is a lot different. Guys are bigger in pro basketball. I never saw so many big people. In college you see a couple of big guys but they don't always have the physical ability that you have. And then in the first days of the pros I went to training camp and saw these big guys, and I was wondering if I really could make it. But right after the first practice I could sense that I was as good as they were. And after the first season with the Lakers I realized I had a lot of talent. I never took it for granted though. I never took the opposition for granted. I just developed and played and never worried about the opposition. I was worried about what I was going to do, how I was going to play, how I was going to react to the situation, and how the team was going to react and play. Everything else, I thought, was going to take care of itself. I knew I was a good athlete then. Each game I just tried to improve upon things I needed to improve on.

As a player I was basically—fundamentally—intelligent. I had the body, the strength, everything to do it. I could probably have made it a lot easier for myself, as I look back, if I faked the game more. But because of the challenge I didn't want to. Guys now have a lot of physical talents but they just play with their bodies instead of their heads. I think basketball is a very simple game if you have any athletic talent, but you have to try to learn the fundamentals of the game, because as the body starts to deteriorate, the mind becomes a bit sharper. It gets tougher getting up for every game, and playing gets tougher. But as the years go by and you get more experience, you play more with your head than with your body. As I got older I was still effective. I still had the same productivity, the same scoring points. It wasn't the type of game that I was accustomed to, but I was able to make the adjustment. I'd say that in the first few years of my career I didn't realize that I was not going to be playing the same way later. But I started thinking about it earlier than a lot of athletes because I had a serious injury.

In 1965, my seventh year, I had a very serious operation. The doctors didn't think that I would play again. They removed part of my kneecap, tendons, ligaments, and so on. This destroyed the knee. I had to play a different type of game and I knew eventually it would come to the point where I would have to retire. I was taught that if you've got a little injury, you play. You've got to learn to play with pain, a bad knee or something. You just go out there and play. I don't know if that's good or bad. I always thought that the doctor, the coach, and the people involved would be fair and honest enough not to send me out there if it would endanger me. But later on I found that this was not so. They were concerned about themselves. I never thought about that until the last two years of my career. Then, when I wasn't really able to play, I started to think about a lot of things. The coach's attitude was that I just didn't want to play. I think that coaches relay this idea to management—that a player's capable of playing but he doesn't want to. So that sort of turned me off. Of course, bitterness was part of it. But the fact was that I was tired of playing. After thirteen years I knew that I couldn't play as well as I once had, and I figured it was time to stop. I guess it was pride, or ego. Knowing that I couldn't perform up to my expectations, it was time.

When I stopped playing, I didn't even think about playing again. It didn't bother me one bit. I can always turn things off when I want to. I don't necessarily say that is a good quality or a virtue, because a lot of times I find myself turning off even when I'm not competing. It was good when I was out there playing. But when one game was over I could forget about that particular game. I didn't stay up all night going over the game. I'd think about the next one.

I wanted to stay in basketball in some capacity after I retired. Basketball is the only thing that I have ever done. It's been my life. Coaching is the most hazardous profession you can be in. It's funny. If you have a winning team, the coach is responsible for the wins, and also responsible for the losses. But I think it's players who win or lose. Coaches put it together, the right chemistry and people, but the players make certain decisions out there. So if you have the talent, you're going to win; if you don't have the talent, you're not going to win. It's as simple as that. It's difficult to know how to handle the players. What really shakes some of the players up—makes them take a good look at themselves and what direction they might be going in—is trading them. No one likes to be traded and I hate to see people moved around, particularly players with families. But that's sometimes the only thing that straightens a player out. It's sad.

A player has to realize his limitations. There's no way you can convince him that there is a possibility he won't be with this particular team next year or he might not even be in basketball next year. You try to tell him what to do to prepare himself if he wants to stay in basketball. A lot of guys have so much confidence in their physical ability that they believe they will have a job tomorrow with some other ball club. It's very difficult.

When I started off as assistant coach I had very little patience with the guys because I expected them to be like me. A lot of players I've been around have their limits. There are certain things they can do, certain things they can't do—but I expected these guys to do everything. I think that's the one thing I've learned—patience. Losing is very difficult. I hate to lose. But once the game is over, even if we lose it, it's over. It's over when the season is over. In the end we're all responsible if we win and we're all responsible if we lose.

Dave DeBusschere

As a kid, you dream. Playing ball in the Detroit Stadium where the Tigers play—I guess it was a fantasy. No, I think it was more of a solid dream, whatever a solid dream is. I guess it was a deep-down desire to become a pretty good professional athlete. I always thought that was the thing to be, but I never thought it would be possible at that time. I knew I was doing well in sports, but how to gauge how well at a young age is very difficult. What do you have to gauge it by?

I always played baseball much more than basketball. I never really thought of becoming a professional basketball player until I started to excel at it in high school. I thought then that maybe I could get a scholarship. My parents couldn't afford to send me to college; there was no way. I could have signed to play baseball. I was doing very well as a pitcher and the scouts came around the house dangling more money. My father, because of his European background and being a laborer all his life, couldn't understand that I could make more money in a year than he saw in ten years. "To throw a baseball and they want to pay you? It's crazy."

But I started to progress in basketball and, I guess through my schooling, I started to realize there was a big world out there. I wanted to prepare myself for it so I chose to go to college. I selected a local school which is a fine university, the University of Detroit. There was a good baseball program there and an excellent basketball program also. In college I started to really think about professional basketball because I could see myslf developing when I started to play against some professional guys, like the Trotters. I knew that I was holding my own with them even though I was just a freshman. That was a sort of barometer by which I could gauge my abilities at that point. Then as a sophomore I played against the college seniors and once again I got an indication of my abilities because some of them went on to play professional basketball. By the time I was a junior I was in a stronger position to judge my own progress. I still didn't know whether to choose baseball or basketball. I had people after me for both sports.

Now basketball was not a major sport in the sixties as it was in the seventies. For example, there were only eighteen teams in basketball *then and it didn't have the national publicity it has now. Maybe in New York it did, but when you got out of New York, it wasn't that big a deal. Baseball was. I didn't know which one I was really going to develop in or do the best in, and since both organizations were willing to let me play the respective sports, even though there was some overlap in seasons, I played both.*

The summer I graduated I played baseball with the White Sox farm team for two months and then with the team for two months. After that I went right into basketball in Detroit where I did fairly well the first year and then nothing. In fact, as far as development, I did better my first year in baseball than in basketball. And then my second year in baseball was kind of a bad year for me because I was new on the pitching staff. They were going after a pennant, so there was little chance for me to pitch. I threw a hundred-something innings that year, won a few games and lost a few, but it was nothing like I had really hoped. When I went back to basketball that year I had the worst season ever. I played fifteen games and broke my leg. I still didn't know what to do so I went back and forth, continuing two careers. I think my third year in basketball I started to move along. By my fourth year I became player-coach. The thing I didn't like in baseball was that as a pitcher, when you didn't pitch you sat around. You sat in the bullpen, chewed tobacco, played password, told stories. I found that boring. They were about to move me into a standing rotation but I was convinced that I had progressed faster in basketball. I guess I liked it better. Also, the dual careers and the responsibility of being a player-coach was too great. I knew that I had to make a decision between the two sports. I chose basketball.

Every coach is on an interim basis. Detroit didn't have anybody at that time to replace the old coach, but they wanted him out. So they asked me to make a decision right away and that would allow them to go out and look for somebody. I said okay. And just after I took the job, we started to win a few games—but that normally happens any time you replace an old coach. After the original impetus wears off it settles back down. I guess we were all naïve enough to think that the winning would continue.

Looking back, these were probably the darkest times of my career because my job was such a heavy burden. The whole idea of player-coach affected me. I worried a lot. We went through major blunders and hardships and just unfortunate circumstances. After I was made player-coach, the general manager of the team died. For a while there was no one to lean on. I was left alone in the professional basketball world at the age of twenty-four and I had no one to work with. It was frustrating. I was left wearing two hats—playing the game plus trying to watch what was going on around me, and trying to count fouls. It was impossible for me to look after everything at once out there. You're responsible for making cuts and at the same time playing with the guys. How do you criticize guys on your own team when you're making mistakes out there yourself? Well, if I had to do it again I doubt that I would take the job of player-coach.

However, it was a tremendous experience for me. I think it helped me understand the game. Every player, even if he only coached for half a *season, would have a different outlook on the game afterward—particularly players who have been somewhat pampered all their lives. Their sole responsibility is to win the game. It's knowing that it's not what they do as individuals, but the fact that the team wins that would help them. It helped me, I know that. But I wasn't mature enough to handle the job. I wasn't able to cope with both aspects. It affected my play on the one hand and my coaching on the other, and I was criticized for both. I couldn't do justice to the sport, the team, or myself, so I quit as a coach. But I continued to play there. That created some problems because having been the coach made it tough on everybody. I played for two years and then, of course, I was traded.*

I didn't know anything about the trade until it was completed. It took place—I don't quite remember—sometime around Christmas. I was home; it was about six-thirty. I got a call from Ed Coyle, the general manager. He said, "You're being traded to New York for Bellamy. We're sorry to do it." And I said, "Gee, I guess there's nothing you can do about it." The ironic thing was that I was just hanging in my den a picture of Bellamy driving a basket with me guarding. A beautiful picture. We were getting the house ready for Christmas. Gerry was pregnant. I said, I guess if I'm traded anywhere, I'm happy to go to New York. That was my total response.

I welcomed the opportunity. I knew New York was a strong club. You know a club is strong after you've played against it. Everybody else always felt that its only shortcoming was the fact that it had two big guys and couldn't use Willis Reed properly. I would have been perfectly happy to play my whole career in Detroit. The trade meant nothing to me except the fact that I was going to a very competitive club.

They called me on a Thursday night. New York was in town and I played with them the following night. I made about nineteen or twenty points. I had feelings! After anybody gets traded and you go back and play against the team that has traded you, there's a certain amount of, I guess, ego. "I'm going to prove to you guys that you were wrong. How could anybody trade me?" But, in all honesty, and maybe it's not the normal way to react, I thought that it made sense for both clubs. Maybe I was just trying to figure it out. I do that.

I sit down and evaluate everything before I get flustered. I try to take my time and appraise exactly what things mean and how they affect me. If you act impulsively you find that you make the wrong decisions. In other words, in a logical process black and white are very easy to distinguish but there is always gray. People who can take the gray part and insert it back into the black and white are the ones, I think, who are prepared. They can make logical sense out of things. Decisions are made in the gray areas. That's the way I look at it.

I hate to see somebody take the gray area and pass it on to somebody else because it tells me something about that individual. On a basketball court that's the guy who won't take the last shot in the game or won't run back to get the ball at the end because he's afraid he might make a mistake. Those are gray areas to me and that's the way I judge people. In a judgment business like basketball I watch the guys in important situations. I look for guys who are willing to take the chance and make the decision to go out and win the game for you. No one blames you if you miss the last shot, you just feel sorry for a guy who does. But if he's unwilling to take the shot, I don't want him on my team because then he hurts us and the team effort.

I feel personally that one of the things that made the Knicks tremendously effective in the years we won the championship—and even in some of the years we didn't—was the lineup. In 1970, and again in 1973, the only difference between the lineup was the replacement of Barnett by Monroe. We replaced a guy who was willing to take the last shot or assist at any time in the play. That was what was tremendously effective in our club, because a team cannot direct the defense to stop a club in those situations. We were effective in the last two minutes of any game because we were all able to take chances. Most clubs have three guys at the most who will take these last second shots. I've never seen a fast break in the last two minutes of a game. There isn't: it's a pattern game. The ball's got to move, there have to be individual movements, and that makes it tough for defense.

It was a chemistry with the Knicks, a blend among the individuals that resulted in communication. Everybody knowing the personalities well

enough so that we could all accept criticism. I could say something to Bradley, or to Willis, Earl, or Clyde. Clyde would really listen. He took it; he absorbed it. We found that when we got those lines of communication open, the willingness to sacrifice to help our team or teammates, not expecting anything in return, was a common goal. We went to win, we were going to perform at our heights. That was fun, really fun.

When you talk about a team concept or a "well-oiled machine" that is an offensive unit, or in football a defensive one, there's no key. The only key is the acceptance of an individual's mentality, starting with a coach and running through the personalities of the individuals on the team. The only thing you have to know is simple. It's the willingness to sacrifice for somebody else's shortcomings or mistakes and to make up for them without expecting anything in return. If you can do that, you've got it made. The rest is downhill.

The fulfillment that I received from basketball came from this whole concept of teamwork. This blend of characters from diverse backgrounds—together in an arena, excluding outside influences and everything else—making it all work. Then, when it works, and it did work to the point where we were tremendously successful. . .fantastic! I was on a natural high.

My private moments did not make it that gratifying. What did was the fact that everything combined made it such an enormously fulfilling experience for me. It was a combination of things coming together at one focal point. But those are memories I cannot describe. Those experiences—the first minute you come into a locker room after winning the championship—how can you share the feeling or describe it to anyone else outside the team or the coach? It's impossible. I can't tell Gerry. I don't know how to explain it. It's like looking somebody right in the eye and having them know what you're thinking. Your communication goes right. You know you've done a good job. You know you're the best in your profession in the whole world. But there is more. It's such a community thing. Those are perhaps the great, great moments. Just a moment when you sort of clench your fists. I think it's like being a woman. She can't share the feeling of having a baby with someone else. It's what *you feel and know and have accomplished. But the feeling goes away; it's there maybe a minute or maybe it will last two or three. But whatever that period is, it's terribly, terribly difficult to explain.*

I didn't switch out of basketball because I had another passion. I just felt deep down that it was time to make a change. I decided that twelve years of what I had gone through was enough. I also knew that I could have played another year, assuming that I would have been repaired in a normal period of time. I had ripped my stomach muscles. I guess history sort of sets the guidelines for you. You reach a certain age and your body doesn't function the way it did before. I knew all along that this day was going to come and I was getting ready for it. You just don't sit back and prepare yourself in one day for something like that. When you start thinking about it, you realize you can't go on forever. There's a whole new life out there. You can go into other things. There are less than three hundred professional basketball players in the United States. If the rest of the population can get by, you can, too.

I didn't sever ties right away. I stayed around the sport—which helped. Becoming general manager of the Nets, I remained involved. I grew away on a more gradual basis. The only time I really missed it that year was when the excitement of the playoffs came around again. It seemed to generate emotions in me. Then even that feeling grew away.

You've got to be realistic about it. It's a very proud feeling you have when you're recognized in a profession, when you've been one of the good or great players, or you've made a great contribution to the sport that you've been involved in. It's very self-satisfying. It obviously opens a lot of doors for you that aren't available to other people. You have to be very thankful for that. But all of a sudden the cheering stops. You've got to go out into the big world and make it on your own. The big, wide wonderful world that you knew as a player isn't the same when you're done playing. You're not as visible as you once were. You find a lot of people who associated with you at one time falling off. They weren't your friends. I tried to be very selective with people. I wasn't interested in a guy who would say, "Come over and I'll give you a suit of clothes." I'm not selling myself to anybody, I don't need that. I wanted to be with peo-

ple who were real, just interested—and you've heard this a million times—in Dave DeBusschere the athlete, as a person.

I'm convinced that whatever I get into I won't be afraid to pay my dues. I've always been willing to do that. I guess the only thing is, I'm driven. I want to get involved in something that's real, that I can get my teeth into, become an important part of. I'm driven by the fact that I can't stand to be bored. If there were a fire, I'd jump in and either put it out or do something to help. I wouldn't want to run around the fire and look at it. Maybe I would get singed, or maybe not. I couldn't stand that! If there's a problem, I think you go into it and try to solve it.

I don't have a dream. As long as I'm mentally satisfied, that's probably the most important thing—to play an active role in something that I'm mentally satisfied with. When you look at it historically, if you're lucky to last till you're thirty-four, that's only half a lifetime. You've still got half a lifetime left to live.

Willis Reed

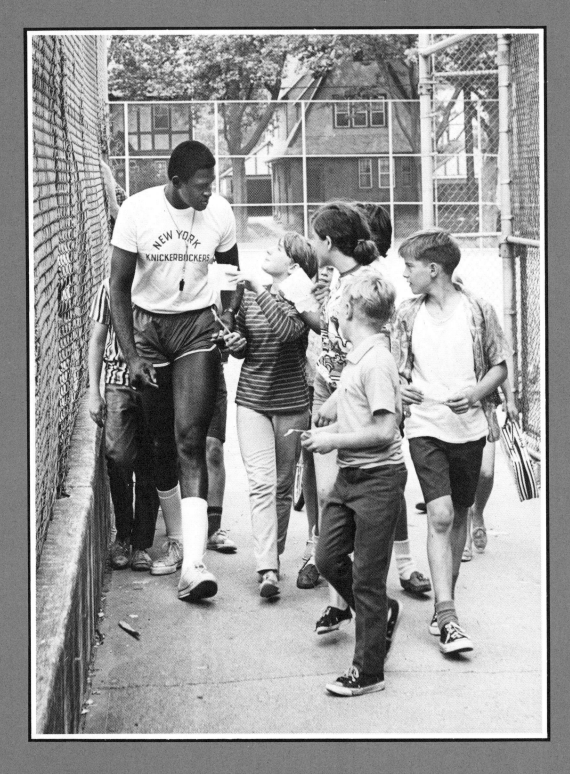

My career ended abruptly as a player, which wasn't by my script. I was an injured player, living out a two-year contract, wanting to play but unable to. It didn't finish by my script for sure.

When people say to me that the most inspirational thing they'd seen in basketball was that game May 8, 1970, they can't really know what was going on in my brain. My whole dream was to play in a championship game against the greatest center in basketball. And I had only one good leg. That was the pinnacle of my career. If I never played another game in my life, I wanted to be out there—even though I couldn't give what I wanted. I kept thinking, why me?

Some man once asked me how I explain to my son that in the biggest game I ever played I only scored 4 points? Well, it wasn't the biggest; it was the most important. It encapsulated my every dream. It was my private moment. Nothing will reach that pinnacle again.

It was exciting for me to know that I could come into a competition trying to beat a Kareem Abdul Jabbar, trying to beat someone who's got the odds in his favor. For me it was super! There were many nights I lay awake wishing I was as good as Wilt Chamberlain or Bill Russell, wishing I could beat them, waiting to beat them. I wanted to be the best. I grew up with the odds against me and I knew I didn't have that certain natural ability to be the best; so any time I could beat those odds, it was ecstasy for me. That was strong motivation.

I don't care how much ability you've got; it's what you do with it that counts. If you can get the most out of yourself you can go to bed at night knowing you've given it all. Anything you make is what you keep. That's my philosophy in life.

I started out wanting to play football. The game is dominated by physical contact and I like that. It appealed to me at that age—like a pretty girl, or something else now. It was masculine. But at the age of thirteen I was 6-foot 5 with a size 13 shoe and my ninth grade coach told me I was going to play basketball. I think my love for football, its physicality, became an asset to me in basketball. I wasn't afraid of getting hurt and I worked to get strong because I knew that a strong body meant better performance and perfection.

Eventually, I knew I was decent at basketball. I could shoot the ball; I was able to run; I could do things some big guys couldn't. There is greater freedom in basketball. You're one thirty-second of the pie in football and one-twelfth in basketball. You're playing both offensively and defensively. And, of course, you've got to talk about the tallest man on the team. He's got to be more valuable than the shortest. There was a decided advantage for me in going into basketball.

When the Knicks drafted me, I was very upset. They drafted me number two and at the time I thought Detroit was going to draft me. The scout for Detroit, Joe Lord, had seen me play some of the best games of my college career and there was no way in the world, I thought, that anybody else would be drafted before me. At that time I wanted to play for Detroit. What I knew then, as a future basketball player just out of Grambling College in 1964, and what I knew in 1974, were two different things.

I played for one team throughout my career. My loyalty as a player and my love for a team will always be with New York. Through good times and bad, whatever I got in my professional life New York provided.

I tripped on playing basketball and watching other guys play. There's nothing more artistic than watching someone like Julius Erving. They say I was a good player, but for physical ability I couldn't carry Erving's jock. He can do things with his body I could never do. To play with a Walt Frazier, Earl Monroe, or Dave DeBusschere—men who consistently did what those men could do—that's artistic. A lot of people may not understand that.

I was a performer and the public had to be happy with my performance of the show. But I did things that probably only satisfied me. I played for all aspects of the game—for the enjoyment of teamwork, the game itself, the money—all those things.

I'm thirty-four years old and I've made more money than I'll ever make again. My business put me through college and fed my family. But we athletes aren't really prepared to retire. Most people my age—lawyers, doctors, whatever—are just getting started. Retirement, that's a real big adjustment. Those last two years when I couldn't play probably would

have been two of the most pleasant, because I had climbed to the top of the mountain, looked over, and seen the valley below. I could have walked down the other side and enjoyed.

A man my age accomplishing his greatest dream is a sad thing. I think a man or woman should always have a dream. I'm looking for something challenging, rewarding, my thing. Well, I'm working on a new dream.

Rick Barry

Everybody is a product of his environment. Mine happened to include a lot of sports. I think if I had been in a home where my parents were musicians, more than likely I would have gone into music. I made the decision in high school that basketball was the one sport I was going to play. I was a baseball player then and had had a bad experience. I was a pitcher and thought I was a good one. I could play every position in the field but they wouldn't let me play when I didn't pitch, so I told them forget it, I don't want to play. From that point on I concentrated my efforts on basketball. Of course, I was preparing myself along the way; if I didn't make it, at least I would have an education.

As a child I wanted to be a millionaire. I would tell my aunt when I'd ride around with her that when I got older I would buy her all the flowers she wanted, because I was going to have a lot of money. I always wanted a lot of everything, and I knew that meant you had to have money. So I've always strived for it. I think it's a goal that anybody can have, really, if you go out and apply yourself.

Basketball was something I liked. My father never pushed me; he just taught me. He was a strict fundamentalist in teaching the game. If I would do something wrong I would be immediately reprimanded for it. I'd be taken out of the game. He would tell me why I was taken out— because I made a fundamental mistake or did something you shouldn't do on the floor, like turning my head and losing sight of the ball. A simple thing; you're supposed to keep a man-ball relationship. Consequently, I learned the game that way and became a perfectionist from the standpoint of the game itself. I think that had an influence on me as a person, too. I said, well, okay, you have to do this thing right, and all that just rubbed off onto other areas when I got older. Evidently there was something in me that made me respond favorably. Some youngsters may have responded negatively.

I'd go out all day long and work on the different fundamentals and practice by myself, whereas the kids now all want to go out and just play. They play with other kids and they don't really practice the things they need to practice. They don't have someone teaching them the proper techniques, the proper fundamentals of team playing, or what the game

really involves. I was fortunate enough to have proper schooling. There are a lot of guys who have much more natural ability than I have. They are bigger; they can handle the ball better. I go to the basket and all of a sudden there's a seven-footer standing in front of me. I've got to try to outsmart him, try to fake some way, and do something to get him out of position so that I can get the ball and maybe get it into the basket.

I think intelligence is part of being a great basketball player. Some guys have great natural ability and they're fine performers, but they get to a certain level and that's as far as they go because they don't have the intelligence. They don't know the game—the basic concepts to make their overall game much better—and how to use their individual skills to improve their performance.

It's no fun losing; I don't enjoy it. It's fun only when you're playing the game the way it was designed to be played. Basketball epitomizes team sports, and that's what it's all about. Within that context, if you are an individual performer at a high level of efficiency, well, then that's the ideal situation. That's what I strive for every time I play. You have to realize what your goal is and you have to be man enough to accept your role, even though it may be something contrary to what you would like to be doing. If that's what the coach feels you should be doing to help the team win, you have to be a little self-sacrificing. It's hard to find that kind of combination. In most teams that win championships, that's what you have.

Sometimes I'm not quite prepared to start a game. My feelings take over and I have to kick myself in the butt to get going and get involved. In my earlier years I had to learn from my mistakes. I'd go over things and say, I'll try not to do this the next time. But I wouldn't get to the point where it would bother me so I wouldn't sleep. It did initially, but I learned not to let it affect me. I've only had three games where it's affected me and I realized it and corrected it. Now I have the ability to block outside interference. I take a problem and put it in the back of my head. I just go out and play. As soon as the ball is thrown up, I just react to it. I'm in a different world when I'm on the floor. I'm playing, that's what I'm into.

But still, it's gratifying only if the team is doing well. There's certainly an individual feeling of satisfaction, but there's a void if I go out and play an exceptionally good all-around game and we lose. That really tarnishes it for me; it's just not gratifying. I don't like to play poorly, but I'd much rather have a poor personal game and have the team win than to have a really outstanding one and have the team lose.

I appreciate fine talent in any field, like Julius Erving. Here's a guy with all this great ability and yet he plays the game the way I think it should be played. He's a team player. I respect him for that. I have certain criteria that I have set for myself as far as my personal performance is concerned—nothing that takes away from the team concept, though. Never in my life have I played a game that I have been totally satisfied with, and I don't expect to. Yet I'll try to play the perfect game, even though I know I never can. In fact, when I was younger it was really a problem, because I would do something wrong and be so upset that I would basically take myself out of the game because I was so mad. Meanwhile, the team was going down the other end of the floor and scoring a basket. It took a long time to keep my feelings under control. When I went to the pros, playing a bad game would still bother me, but I learned very quickly. Fortunately, the thing that you have in pro basketball is that you really have to learn very quickly. You don't have time to mull over all the problems and sit back, because the next night you have another game and you have to go out there and prepare yourself for it. So for the type of person I am, it's a blessing in disguise.

I just can't stand mediocrity. I feel that if I do something incorrectly, that's mediocrity and I can't stand it. I know that I'm better than that. It annoys the hell out of me. Part of it is that I'm a perfectionist. I try to take as good care of myself as I can. But I'm also realistic enough to know that as I get older I can't do the same things that I could do five years ago, so I make adjustments. It gets to the point where a plateau comes, where all of a sudden your body starts to break down. The intelligence side of it can compensate for some of the physical deficiencies that you acquire. Up to a point you can still perform at a level that is personally acceptable, but then all of a sudden, because of the physical aspects of the

game, you get to the point where you deteriorate in such a way that you can't compensate mentally. That's the time you've got to get out.

Basketball is entertainment, but not to the point where you think about the fact that you're going out there to make an audience laugh. The fact that people want to come out and watch me play is, I think, super. I love to play and I'm being paid to go out and do the best job I can to help the team win. I love it from that standpoint because I have a chance to go out there and show what I'm capable of doing—to use the abilities that God gave me. I'm very fortunate. We are all very fortunate. That's one of the reasons that I'd rather get out while I'm at the top of the game, so I can look back and have people say, "He could have played a couple of more years," rather than saying, "He ought to get out."

I always believe in preparing myself. I've studied to become a broadcaster. I worked ever since I was out of college and I was in the pros in radio and broadcasting. I worked at it. I paid my dues, as they say. So I don't think I'm getting anything I don't deserve. There are things in life that you get because you're Rick Barry, the basketball player.

I enjoy notoriety. My image is important but I know I can't please everybody, and I'm not going to change everybody's opinion of me, whatever I do. I understand that. I live with it and just have to accept it, but it still bothers me. When I walk off the court I forget about Rick Barry, the basketball player, and become Rick Barry, the person. I've separated the two, though not totally, because people who see me in public only see Rick Barry, the player. I just go out and do whatever I feel like doing. I don't let this deter me.

I don't want to make a fool of myself; that would annoy the hell out of me. I realize, if I'm going to try something I haven't prepared for, I'm liable to make a fool of myself. What I would do is find some way, somehow, to get an opportunity to go out and do whatever it is I did again and prove that I can do it. I would never accept defeat. The drive to be the best just brings out the best in me.

Basketball is but a means to an end for me. It's not my whole life. As far as I'm concerned, my career is ahead of me. I will become better known five years after I stop playing basketball than I ever was in all the years I played. There's just no question about it. Anytime I get the feeling that I've reached a pinnacle in my life, I'm in trouble. I figure there are always better things ahead. I honestly believe that I can be successful at anything that I make up my mind to be successful at.

It's not a dream. Well, I guess you could dream it, but I know it will be a reality. It's that I dream of being successful in the other fields that I choose to go into. I have the confidence in my own abilities to be successful. If it ever came down that I wasn't, it would probably be a very crushing thing to me. But I'm sure I could handle it. I would find something. I'm a very optimistic person.

Earl Monroe

I started playing basketball at about age fourteen, which is rather late. Before that time I wasn't really into sports that heavily. I lived in Philadelphia in a neighborhood with nothing but gangs, and because I was taking piano lessons I used to get beat up for that, not so much by the guys from my neighborhood as by guys from other places. If they hadn't seen you around they beat you up because you were new to their neighborhood. I had to quit piano lessons, but there was a dance school on Broad Street so I used to go there. I was the only one from my neighborhood down there, but it was a lot of fun.

I get a big thrill out of putting people together and then seeing them out there and seeing what kind of reaction they get. I sense it's a reaction to me, an extension of me. If it's disapproval, I can see where it comes from and I can make it better eventually. If it's cool I can still see certain things that could be better, but I get a big thrill out of it.

I have a passion for music. I don't play anything. I don't sing. I was in shows in Baltimore. I used to sing in a group and we made a couple of records in the early sixties but I found that I wasn't really the type of guy to be out in front of a lot of people making funnies. I had too many little quirks. But I have a passion for putting acts together and seeing them grow.

When you're fourteen and 6-foot 3 you automatically have to play some kind of sports, so that's what happened. I was primarily interested in soccer and baseball. The only reason I really got into basketball was because I am the same height now and only 6 pounds heavier than I was at fourteen, so the coach automatically brought me out for basketball. I wasn't good at first and I think that more than anything else this was one of the things that spurred me on. There I was in the schoolyard and the guys I'm growing up with aren't picking me to play. I'm the only guy who's left and all of a sudden they say, "Well, there's no place left to play him." It just spurred me on to play basketball. It seems as though most of the things I've acquired and done in my lifetime always came out of that same premise—having to prove something to somebody.

In the first couple of years in high school I played soccer, then I switched to basketball. From then on I wanted to be a basketball player.

I didn't go to college right away because I thought that I was good enough to play professionally when I got out of high school. I was going to try for the ABL Philadelphia Tapers, which is the league that preceded the ABA back in 1962. Just before I was supposed to go and try out, the league folded. That was in October. I stayed out of school for a year, then went to prep school for a little while, got disenchanted with that, and went to work in a factory. After one year I decided that it wasn't the thing for me, so I went to school the following September.

I went to Winston-Salem in North Carolina on a work-aid scholarship. They didn't have the big money to write off guys going to school—most of the guys who went there had to pay all or part of their tuition. I worked for my room and board mopping floors in the gymnasium. I didn't start playing basketball right away like I thought I should. I used to call home every week or so and tell my mother to send me some money so I could go home, but she never did. She'd say, "Stick it out another week, call me back and let me know how it's going." Finally, after the basketball season was over I got into a little riff with my coach—the first time I cursed at an adult. He said, "Do you know what you just said to me?" I said, "Yes sir, and I'm sorry." He said, "I'm not going to forget that. When you become a success I'm going to bring that back to you and let you know that using your aggression to play well was the way to go." It turned into a great big love affair. I had a stepfather while I was growing up. So when I went to college my coach became a father image for me and after that first year, and for the remaining three years, it was a very close relationship, and next year as a sophomore I started on the team.

When I got out of college, the scout for the Baltimore Bullets didn't want to draft me because he had just seen one game that I played. I got 22 points but they were double- and triple-teaming me and we lost. They sent another guy out to the Pan-American trials, and I did the whole thing—assists and all that nonsense. But the ironic thing about it was that everybody got picked for the Pan-Am team except me. The scout saw enough out there though, so I was the second person picked by the pro draft. Nobody knew me and being the second pick, I went back to proving myself again. I became rookie of the year.

I forced the trade when I left Baltimore for New York. I simply told them that I wouldn't play for them anymore. I gave them three cities, Chicago, Los Angeles, and Philadelphia. And I was going to the ABA if I couldn't get anything. It just happened New York wanted me. I was going out to make a deal with Indiana and then I got the word from New York. I went back to playing against the best players. I should have gotten over that when I got out of college but I still felt that competitive urge and I felt the best players were in the NBA. I went back to proving myself.

Of course, when I came to New York it was a different type of setup. In Baltimore we were a running team. Having that freedom of expression leads to being something of a soloist, yet within the team training. You really don't have to know the game of basketball to appreciate the things that are done beautifully.

I don't know what I'm going to do when I'm on the court. I let a player commit himself and as he commits himself over here that means I've got to go over there; as he tries to trick me and go over there, that means that I'm going to have to come around this way. I get a big thrill out of doing those things. Sometimes I surprise myself. Sometimes when I move I do something and in the midst of doing it I say, damn, Earl. I get a good feeling from that because I might be doing some physical thing I haven't done in a long time. That's part of the thrill of playing now in New York. Being regimented for so long, I had all this pent-up energy. I didn't have any release for it. Now a lot of it has come out again. It's like one of those good old feelings that you used to have and all of a sudden you find it again and it's just that much warmer, to me at least.

I've always had a temper and as I grow older it's one thing I really have learned to control. I think if I accomplish nothing else in my lifetime, that's one of the major obstacles I've tackled. It comes back now and then. It's good for me to play with a temper, especially with the Knicks, because we're a team that gets very passive. Everybody is kind of cool and we don't have any of that real fight in us. Everybody seems to push us over. I feel when I expand myself I get a little more fight in me and it kind of circulates around the team. When I get a little incensed it makes the other guys a little angrier and we're all a little more aggressive. It's a

controlled type of anger, a calculated thing. I might get a technical at the beginning of the game. It's only seventy-five dollars, which actually adds up in the long run, but what it does during the game is make the referee aware of what's happening out there.

My main concern is trying to win the game and make everybody happy. I try to keep the other guys' spirits up, especially the younger guys who have a tendency to do something that might not be called for and they might be reprimanded for. I want to pat them on the behind or something, and say, "It's okay, it will work out better next time." Those things add more to a guy's performance than a lot of things that are shown in the record books. Showing them that somebody else believes in them can be more of a booster than swallowing 1000 points a game. If there's anything I can do on the court that's positive for the team, eventually it's going to be positive for me.

I'm kind of a hard person to satisfy. I guess I'm just like that record, "More and More and More." I want to do more, and although basketball offers security and all that, I think there's a lot more I can do—not only in basketball but in what I can derive from basketball. I want to be right on the brink of that. What I really want is two successful careers at once. Basketball is a big part of my life, but it's a part I can do without. I found that out this year more than any other year. It was the first time that I haven't played any basketball at all after the season, and I only played two or three times passively before training camp. The rest of the time I just played tennis. This was the first year that I really wasn't happy to go back and play basketball, I could have just stayed out. So I feel I should be doing something else. I'm pretty well-rounded and can do a lot of things, so I want to try to do some of those things.

I want to get into acting—television acting, guest star appearances. From that a lot of things may grow—producing, maybe even directing. I think if I can get two careers going for me like that, I can open up a lot of doors not only for myself, but for people who follow me. You know, I think that the help you give to another person eventually is going to come back and help you. It's like putting the pieces together to make the whole and eventually that's what should happen if everything works out all right. If it doesn't work out, okay. You can't blame yourself. You just have to keep going and try harder.

Earl Monroe

I'm a loner but I still enjoy entertaining people. I like to make people laugh. I like to make people think that they belong. I try to exhibit it in all the things I do; playing basketball is only one. When I got to New York I became regimented but it also did a lot of things for me. It put me in a back seat and let me look at everything else that was happening. I didn't want to cause any type of dissension and I didn't want guys to think that I came here to take over their jobs or anything like that. I came here to be part of a team. And eventually we're all going to be paid. This is New York and if anything goes wrong, word is going to spread and you'll be labelled throughout your career—or your career might just end.

I guess one of the things I've been trying to squash for so long is that people think I'm a hot dog. I've known too many guys who leave here and have good careers. So it's part of a learning system, learning what's happening and then going out and trying to act upon it. Guys talk about going to New York because it's the land of opportunity. You get all the commercials you want to do, you make all your business acquaintances, and all that kind of stuff. But it's actually a farce because those opportunities are only open to certain guys. I say, play your cards, just cool it out. Eventually those opportunities will be cool for you, but what you want to do is see exactly where you're going first. So I'm trying to get everything together so that I can just stop playing and do whatever I want to after that.

I've always been someone to pick up on a lot of things just to be able to say, I can do this. I won't miss the physical aspect of basketball because I'll be a tennis player. At thirty-two, tennis took the place of everything else physical. It's strange how that happened. I picked it up again last year, and last summer it just took me. I'm going to buy some land in Jersey so I can put a little cabin and a tennis court out there. That's all I want now. I want to be good; I want to be really good. Tennis is very competitive; you have to have the killer instinct in order to be any kind of a winner, and that comes out in me. It's all me way deep down inside. I'm kind of a passive type of person and I don't really show most things that bother me. When I show a fit of anger on the court, I want to show it, and that's true in every facet of what I do in life, over and over again. Something like playing tennis. It's all killer.

Walt Frazier

As a kid I had no dreams, no idols. I was always a doer. I never liked to go window-shopping because I never wanted to see something that I couldn't get. Why tempt myself. I thought basketball was fun. When I was in high school I played it mainly for the attention of the girls, then, for an education, I played in college. My first years in the pros I played for money. But now I play for pride. Pride means everything to me right now. Anybody who plays a sport has to have pride if they want to be the best.

I was the oldest member of a large family. I have seven sisters, and till my younger brother was born, I was the only boy. At first we had everything we wanted. We used to go shopping every Saturday. Then all of a sudden we didn't go shopping anymore. My father suffered a financial setback and it kind of tripped him out. So he wasn't around as often; he wasn't an influence in the family. It was mostly my mother. We were raised very leniently. The girls had no curfews and I never had one after I was thirteen. But I never went astray. I played with guys sixteen or seventeen and was always the youngest. There were times when the guys would gamble and smoke, but if I tried to stay around they would run me home. They'd say, "You're going to be an athlete."

All the kids just enjoyed sports, that was the thing to do in the playgrounds. We always played football, basketball, baseball, Ping-Pong, whatever. I liked them all. When I was playing football I liked that the best. When I played basketball I liked that the best. I always wanted to be a professional athlete. At first I liked football but I was a quarterback and at the time there were no black quarterbacks in football, so I didn't want to take the chance of not being able to play. I also didn't feel I had the speed to make the adjustment if they tried to change me to another position. In high school I was 6 feet 4 and 185 pounds, but really not that strong. I played sports a lot, but as a kid I never had a hard physical job so I never developed a muscular body. My mother never wanted me to play football because it was too rough. Finally, though, she relented and I played it. She never followed the game too closely until one of my sisters became a majorette. Then she came to watch me play. She didn't mind basketball but I think she only attended maybe one or two basketball games when I was in high school.

From the beginning our teachers always taught us that whatever we did we should be the best. "If you're a street sweeper, or a garbage man, be the best." So we had in our minds that whatever we did was supposed to be the best. Now that I'm grown up I don't necessarily agree with that. I think it puts added pressure on kids. Kids with their parents constantly pushing them, wanting them to be a Monroe, me, or somebody else—I don't believe in that. I think if a kid has the talent it's good to encourage him. But don't keep stressing it as if he had to become like Frazier or someone great. I think it's a turn-off for the kid.

There was never pressure from my family to excel in sports. In the eighth grade I played basketball. In the ninth grade all the coaches were telling me to come out for football or for basketball. They knew I had talent; when I played on the eighth grade basketball team I was the leading scorer and rebounder but I still didn't feel I was ready to play in the ninth grade. Every day they would keep pestering me about coming out but I didn't. Finally in the tenth grade I decided I was ready, and I wanted to play. Then I started to play football, baseball, and basketball. I took my own time. I enjoyed all of them. I just didn't want to play at first. It was only when I got to college that I decided I liked basketball the best.

I think because everybody was pushing me, wanting me to come out— it turned me off. Mostly I've never been pushed. Off the court I'm a loner, and when you're a loner there's no one to push you. You don't have that many friends around who will do it. You're on the outside. You're looking at everybody else so you know when to make your move, what you want to do. So it's not a situation where I've ever been pushed to do anything. I went to college because I thought it was the thing to do. The college I went to never recruited me. I just happened to go there. It was like an accident.

I think I saw college as a savior for my family. I could set an example for my sisters; if I went, then maybe they would follow. There were a lot of times that I wanted to quit. It was very difficult coming from a black environment into a white environment. I was behind in a lot of subjects. I couldn't express myself, so I dreaded going to speech or English classes. My first year was rough. I think without sports I would have quit. Luck-

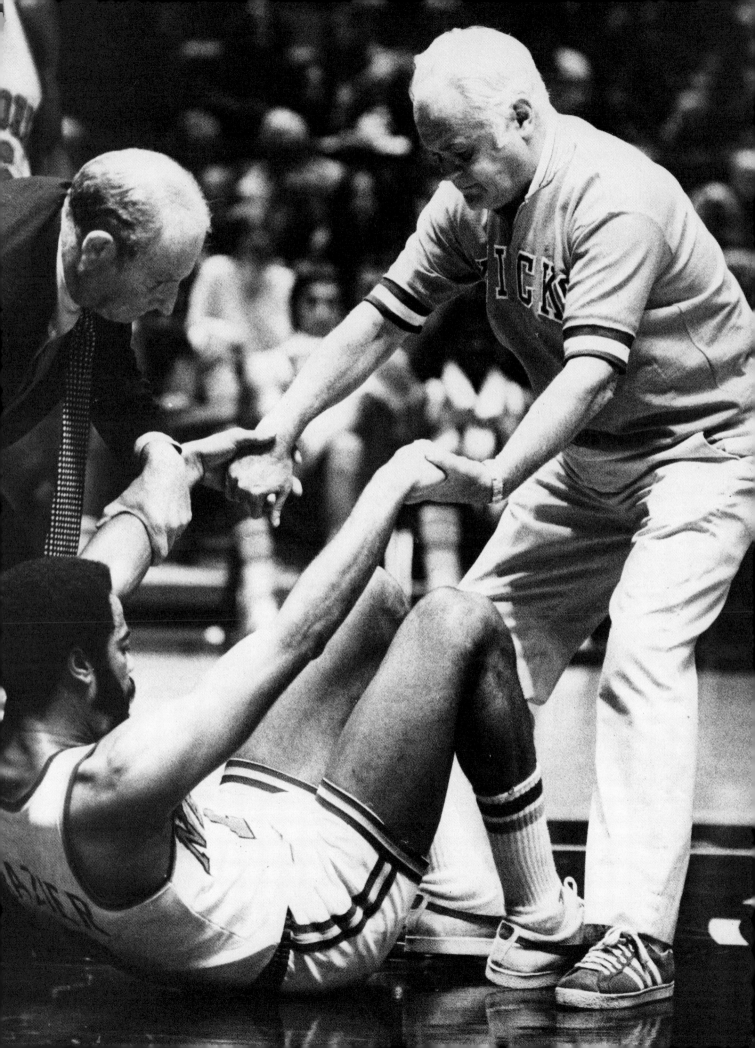

ily, I was having a good season as a freshman. I became a celebrity. People started to help me out and it made it a little easier. But other than that, a lot of nights I just wanted to go home. A lot of nights I cried. Being able to help my family and making my mother proud of me—it was everything. That was the whole thing—and it made me stick it out.

Then the team I played on started to win. There was a deal being made where I was supposed to go to Seattle. Then we came to New York for the National Invitation Tournament. The Knicks possibly would have never drafted me, but fortunately I became the most valuable player of the tournament. As a result I was drafted by New York. It was an accident, so in a way my whole life seems as if it was predetermined.

From the age of thirteen on I never asked my mother for anything. I knew we had less money. I would go to work and I had to know how to clean and wash and care for babies. I think it made me a complete person. I was sort of the man of the house. I was put in a leadership role. In football I was a quarterback. When everybody else was upset I couldn't show that I was. I had to come in the huddles and call the plays. In baseball I was the catcher, leading the team and calling the plays—again in a position of leadership. All these things have played a part in my destiny.

Material things don't mean as much as they used to. I guess they never do once you acquire them. I send money to my mother and sisters. I know they're really going to enjoy the surprise. That makes me happier than anything else that I might do in life—being able to help them out. The happiest moment was when I bought my mother a house. When we lost our money my mother would always see other people's homes and say, "I wish I had a big kitchen." So I said to myself, I've got to do that for her. When I did do it, everything was complete. That's the happiest I've ever been. It was like icing on the cake. Becoming a star, playing in New York—I dwelled on that in my mind for a long time, and I found peace. Maybe that was the only dream I ever had—to be an athlete and to buy my mother a house. I don't know of anything else that I want right now.

With age your goals are different; you mellow. When I started out I wanted to be known. I liked reading my name in the papers. I liked it when I walked down the street and heard people saying, "Hey, that's

Walt Frazier.'' But now I really don't get turned on by that. In the final analysis, in the back of my mind, I want people to like me as a person and not for what I do. At the beginning you think they all love you just for you, but I found out early in high school that it's for what you do.

I was a quarterback in the tenth grade. I was second string and the guy on the first string got hurt, so for six games I was the starting quarter-back. I had no experience and we lost all the games badly. The whole school blamed me. Then basketball season came, I was a star, and every-body loved me again. So I found out how fickle the fans can be. "The thrill of victory and the agony of defeat.'' How the fans turn back and forth.

Then when you go to college it's the same. When you go in they love you; when you lose nobody comes around. That fickleness reinforced what I had already learned in high school. Coming to the pros it was the same thing. The Knicks were losers my first year, but then they started to win and the place was packed, people were going crazy. When we're on a downer I know that people fade away. The scar was imprinted on me since high school and I've always kept a certain distance from the fans. They say "Walt Frazier'' and I acknowledge them, but deep in my heart I don't really let them get too close to me. I'm a professional now. I'd play the same way if nobody showed up. That's my job.

Once basketball was my whole life but last season, when I had such a hard time with injuries when my back went, I was anxious to find ways of strengthening it other than with weights. It was a blessing in disguise because I found Yoga. It's something that I can relate to forever, and I think I will. It gave me a different outlook on life. It's now something that I can do religiously every day—when I wake up in the morning, when I go to bed at night. I've changed my whole act—I take vitamins, I cook for myself, eat lightly. I don't dissipate a lot so I feel really strong. It hap-pened to me before when I lost weight. From 204 I went to 196 and I got quicker and could jump a little faster. It sort of threw me off for a little while. I felt too strong. I couldn't even control my body. I was too quick for myself. I felt so light and my relfexes were so fast I couldn't adjust to them sometimes. It feels like you're out of kilter. You're moving too fast for yourself.

Coming off last season I lost some confidence. This season I was just as confident because I figured I was back! I was really in good shape. I was even better than I was last year or earlier in my career. Some of the guys on the team have different injuries. I know certain things about the body that might help them. Most guys don't realize that they don't know anything about their bodies. They rely on doctors. Doctors are human; they can make mistakes too. So I've learned to do something about my body. It is a business. In basketball your body is your business. So it's important to know what's going on with it. I could talk about the body all day with someone. It would be really interesting. I think when this is over I would like to dedicate myself to helping others, primarily the kids.

Right now, if I had to leave basketball, I'd be perfectly happy. Till now my life has been complete, and if I could do it all over again, I don't know anything or anybody else that I would like to be other than myself. I've had a good career. How many guys play ten years? How many guys become stars of the NBA? I have only good memories about basketball, but I know there are other things in life. Basketball is just a means to an end. When I was growing up, when I went to high school and I had to leave high school for college, I cried and said I'll never have that much fun again. Then I found college was better. So when I left college I said, wow, I'll never have that much fun again. The pros were better. So I'm sure after this is over something else will come along that will be even better.

Bill Bradley

I grew up in a small town in the Midwest. There were three thousand people in the town and most of them worked in factories. My father was a banker there. I was big early in my childhood, and it was assumed that every boy who was big played basketball. I always felt I was different. I didn't feel part of any institution that I was ever in, because from a very early age I had a kind of split life. Until I was thirteen my parents took me to Florida for two months every winter. There I was enrolled in a private school that was totally different from my school in Missouri—and at the other end of the economic pole.

I selected basketball over baseball because I liked it better. It was something you could really get into, really be active in, as opposed to standing in the sun shagging flies. In baseball, at about fourteen, they start throwing curves. I couldn't hit them, so I struggled for a while but I didn't stay with it. I decided to concentrate instead on basketball. In Palm Beach the sports were soccer and fencing, not basketball, so I found a schoolyard and went to play there against all the kids from other schools. It was very awkward for me; there were no real friendships. I would go to the schoolyard and be the first to arrive and the last to leave. I didn't have any friends who stayed there with me for a few hours or who I would see later; so my life was going to school, practicing, going home, eating and studying, and practicing again. The court really became a source of enjoyment—not one of the few, but the only source of enjoyment in an environment that was not entirely comfortable.

I had this split existence until I was thirteen, when I decided not to go to Florida with my parents each winter but to stay home with an aunt and uncle and play basketball. I think that high schools in the Midwest, as well as grade schools there, have a certain place for the athlete. You get feedback from your classmates; there's a certain deference and respect—also from townspeople, adults you don't know, and so forth. You can get all kinds of gratification on many different levels.

That experience was very intense for me, almost to the exclusion of everything else. I used to have great imagination on the court because I would always practice alone. I would imagine situations so that I could continue to stay out there for an hour or two. I'd develop games with my-

self. It would be the last three minutes of a game and I would have to make 3 baskets, which meant we won three games. And I'd have to hit 10 out of 13 in order to make the winning record. Also, I watched the pros play and I would imitate certain moves they'd make. Choreography, basically, was what I was doing. I had been shown certain moves and just repeated them hundreds of times until they became part of my repertoire and until I could do them, reacting without thinking.

When I got into high school, the basketball coach was also the football coach. I didn't play football, so I had to play doubly hard to prove that although I didn't play football I could still be a basketball player. I did that. Working twice as hard contributed to my becoming a pro, as did my earlier experiences with basketball coaches, whom I found to be more authoritative figures—figures I could respect and to whom I deferred. There was also an element of enjoyment in the game—just pure enjoyment and a way of proving myself to all kinds of people—so it was also a source of confidence in my early adolescence.

My childhood was very disciplined in the sense of what I was allowed to do. In my home the concept of a pro athlete was one of a guy who, by the age of thirty-five, was a wreck. After I reached adolescence I had to doctor all these values for myself and apply them without any kind of parental suggestion. As a result there was one side of my personality that developed—the creative, artistic side—through basketball and the more disciplined and rational side through my home and my schoolwork. Both held equal importance for me, but if there was one that held more importance in the home, it was certainly schoolwork. However, the two were intermixed, so the way I approached basketball could be viewed as a very ordered approach. Some of the things I would do in school, what I would write in papers, what I would choose to read or whatever, could be considered artistic and creative.

After a few years it wasn't a matter of proving myself physically against the other players, because I was really superior to them. I was playing against the most formidable foe of all—the imagined foe. In my own mind, that foe was some person in the United States. I had to practice, practice, practice. If I didn't, somebody else out there would be practicing and he'd beat me when we met. And so I had to continue in order to be ready. I kept repeating this over and over in my head, and it was really quite a motivating force.

I think that basketball is one of the sports where there is a chance for creative spontaneity within the context of disciplined group achievement. I don't think it's only in the mind. I think that one of the beauties of the game is that it allows for individual action while at the same time requiring an uncommon sharing and an uncommon mutual sacrifice for the betterment of the whole group. If there's only the ordered robot kind of approach that you get in football, then you have none of the enjoyment of personal expression that you can perform and receive within the context of a team game.

My opinion, in fact, is that you're really seen at your best whenever you can blend your talents effectively with others'. In team sports, it's the whole group that counts. The soloist never really achieves the best of all possible rewards from the game. No soloist ever senses that. Thus, a soloist might indeed be known as a star or an all-star and be paid a large amount of money, but he can never have what I think is the highest feeling—team championship.

One of the anomalies of basketball as entertainment is that the performers never really acknowledge the crowd in a direct or open way. In fact, we are taught from a very early age to ignore the crowd, which is an impossibility. Some players do succeed in that to varying degrees. While in the audience of other kinds of performances I've had chills up my spine when the performer has acknowledged the audience in an open way—when he has received the warm waves of applause and been really carried away by the whole thing himself. What I've seen there is an experience I have never had in the game of basketball because of the nature and code of conduct that surrounds it.

What you do—your work—that's the only thing that gives life some meaning. The other things you look upon as the motivation for your actions, either a monetary reward or public acclaim, are not real. Certainly the money is real and to a certain extent so is a form of acclaim, but they're not the main motivating forces. I think the motivations are the

realization that you enjoy doing what you do and that they are essential to your personality and your own being. So you've brought all this together and you've achieved the highest reward and the highest feeling of accomplishment that your profession offers, which is the championship. Then it's gone in twenty-four hours. By the next day, after you've had some sleep, it's kind of diluted. Even two or three days later when you look back, you reproach yourself because it is a kind of nostalgia. You're being forced to look ahead—to look ahead to next year—to the same kind of work, the same opportunity for the feeling that lasts only a few hours. You play again so that you can have that feeling, but the real truth is that you play again because you like to play and because your work is what's important. Even at its most rewarding, I think there is inherent in the enjoyment the shortness of it. This is not something you know at twenty-three or twenty-five. At that age you play for a lot of jumbled reasons that you don't really sort out. And even if you work at it, you don't sort them out till your late twenties. But one particular aspect of this profession is that by the time you've finally sorted them out and you can acknowledge your enjoyment of the game, it's over.

The end of a career is an unknown. The athlete has to continue living without the game. You stop in your mid-thirties and you suddenly realize you have not faced up to the major questions of identity that most of your peers struggled with in late adolescence or certainly by their late twenties. That's true for most athletes; even if you have struggled with those things and gotten a strong sense of your own identity apart from the game, you still have the fear of the unknown that awaits you at the end of your career. Not only does a career change, but life changes—what you do, how you define yourself.

My life is an example of this to a certain extent. Because of the necessary specialization that's required in my field to reach the top, you can only do it alone. Because of the nature of the business, which forces you to travel in unfamiliar circumstances and sterile environments, it is also true. All these forces promote a sense of isolation. You don't want to extend yourself to other people or go out and interact with them. I felt, here I am on the road; I'm dealing with the sense of aloneness, and I say that I

would like my life to be fuller. In this kind of environment it's a struggle to stay in touch with life's subtleties.

The end is an unknown. You don't know what you'll do. It's a different kind of experience. Take the things that I'm interested in doing, say politics, maybe business, TV, or whatever. One of the things that I have to be sure of—and I am sure of—is that I don't want to go into any other profession seeking the same kinds of rewards in a personal sense that I have received from basketball. In other words, when I see a politician giving a speech to five thousand people before a chicken dinner, I know several things—partly because I've done that as a politician, and partly because I'm a basketball player. One thing I know is that he is in a very lonely position out there. In fact, it is a sort of performance. What he receives from it are votes and contributions and also maybe confirmation that he is a valuable human being. I don't want to go into politics for those reasons. If I do go into politics, I think it will be for the right reasons and not for the attempt to recapture the thrills of twenty thousand people at center court in Madison Square Garden. Finally, I don't know how I'll react.

Kareem Jabbar

The only thing my parents stayed on me about was academics. I wouldn't practice the piano when I was seven or eight. I didn't mind going to my lesson, but when it came time to practice, I'd just rather be outdoors. My parents didn't think it was smart to force me to practice, so I just got into whatever there was to get into.

My father had played lots of sports in high school and he took me with him when he played handball. That's how I got interested in sports and I just stuck with it. I was into everything up to eighth grade. I was on four or five teams. I tried to play as many sports as I could, although I wasn't overwhelmingly good at any of them. But still, during that time I was becoming a pretty good all-around athlete. Watching the 1960 Olympics really motivated me a lot. For the rest of the summer, I remember, I went to the pool to practice swimming when it was open. Seeing it on TV, I wanted to go to the Olympics. The whole glamor of it . . . I was all jazzed up.

Until that time I'd grown a lot faster than my coordination had developed. I was still very awkward. I was a fair athlete. I started playing basketball most of the time and stopped just about everything else. I liked football, but my father threatened me if I played anymore. He didn't want me to get hurt. I had already gotten basketball scholarship offers to high school when he told me, "Don't play football anymore." So I just said, "Forget about football." It wasn't a hard decision.

Being the height I was and being able to play basketball just started to send things my way. Adolescence is a hard adjustment. By the time I was in the ninth grade I guess I was halfway through it, and the awkwardness was leaving me by then. There wasn't anything about basketball that seemed negative, so I just went into it and it started doing things for me. In the ninth grade I was already starting to get college offers. So basketball became a tool for achieving a few things. All the passion that was involved was usually worked out among my peers. Playing every Saturday afternoon in the playground with everybody watching—that was gratification. My most satisfying moments usually came at those times. I went on to become high school all-American, but just being able to do something well in front of all my friends was the biggest joy. I really got a big

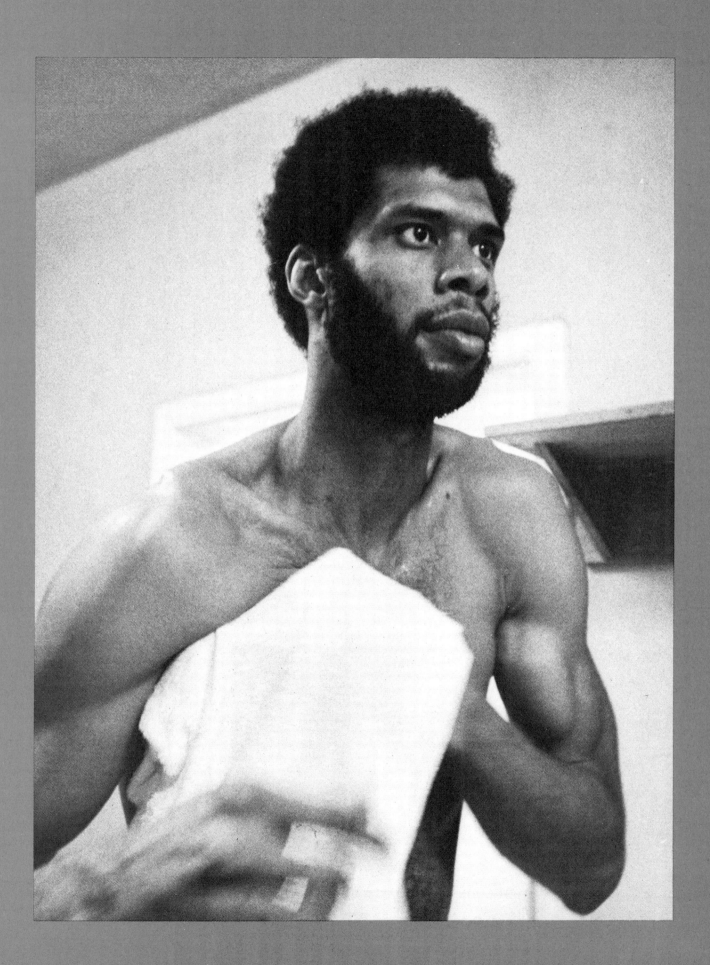

kick out of it. Between eighth and ninth grade I'd always been the clumsy kid in the neighborhood, and here I was doing things that other people couldn't do. It was very gratifying.

At this point in life I relate to the game differently. Being an adult and wanting to do things that adults do, you see your job in a much different light than you would if it was just something that you liked to do. I definitely see it all more clearly now. I'm more mature. The river's changed and I've changed. There are hundreds of thousands of people in this country who play basketball and they can go down to the Y and do it. But to do it on the level that I do, that's another ball game. I could be playing ball and get gratification just out of playing ball; but as far as earning a living and using basketball to better my life, there's only one place I can do that. Right now I feel that whatever liabilities there are to it, it beats the hell out of a nine-to-five job. I see friends of mine, guys younger than me, who have a gut and no hair, who're really wrapped up in the whole workaday thing. Their growth has stopped. They reach a certain level in their lives and that's it. I don't feel confined like that. Maybe it's just my own personal outlook, but I wouldn't trade my job for anything.

My father wanted to get a job as a musician, but in 1952 they just didn't hire classically trained black musicians. He became a cop instead; that was that. I wasn't old enough to realize what that meant. I never remember hearing him cry about it or thinking he'd been victimized. He just went about doing what he could do. I have the ability to be free. I get to see a large part of the country. I've been around the world. I've met people. Basketball has opened up all that for me. And the money benefits have been spectacular. My father worked very hard all his life. He doesn't have very much to show for it. I'm way ahead of the game right now.

I remember feeling resentment in school because I was put in a special class because of my color. Coming to grips with that and learning how to understand can be a problem. That's when I started questioning. I think I've survived it. It has a lot to do with my philosophy of life. I try to appreciate my size and my abilities as blessings and to use them in the most advantageous way I can. Some people have that ability, that "it," *and some people don't, and you can't figure out exactly what it's about. There's no rhyme or reason to it. I try to do the best job I can and have a very big effect on the game, hopefully to the detriment of the team I am playing against.*

Once the game starts I'm pretty much into it, and I know whether I'm physically on or off. I don't worry about my body; it's mainly mental. Once you reach a certain level of physical conditioning and you play the game as long as I have and you have the instincts for the game, it just really depends on whether or not you're applying yourself mentally. Basketball is my profession; it's my life now. It's hard to separate the two. This is what I do, and I do it very well. It's become like breathing or putting on your right shoe first—just part of what you do and part of what you are.

I've never thought of myself as being one-dimensional. That idea comes to me from my parents. They were glad I was able to excel at sports, but their main concern was academics. I've always had it pointed out to me that nothing ever stays the same. After eight years of this I know that for a fact, so I'm not going to the end with any blinders on. I have a lot of things in my mind. I don't know if I'll be able to do any of them, but I'd like to try. I've observed other people I've known and admired who have played the game and are through with it now. Some have survived and some haven't. That all depends on the individual and how you approach it. I guess I'm a difficult subject because I'm more or less a mystic. I just accept things as they come. I don't agonize over things. They happen and that's that. A lot of good has happened to me and I accept it. I've tried to get the most positive feedback out of it that I can. If it should change, I would be very happy that the good things have occurred at all and I could live with that. I wouldn't have any problems living with whatever happened. It's just the way I am. In one way or another I've always been outstanding, always been singled out: the tallest in my class, the only Afro-American in grade school, and after school, as an athlete. Being singled out was a certain distinction accorded me when I was born. I was the biggest baby in the hospital. It's always been like that.

Nate Archibald

I never imagined I was going to be a professional basketball player until I was drafted and stepped into my first pro game. The coach from University of Texas, Don Haskins, saw me play a high school championship and offered me a scholarship. I don't think I was ready to go, but I felt that in order to improve myself I had to go out of state. I had to get into another environment and get accustomed to new living conditions, and that's what I did.

I got drafted by the Cincinnati Royals. I had to go to camp, but I still had to work and still had doubts in my mind. I didn't know at that time whether I could play in the league because of my size and limited experience. Some people have the ability to play but don't know how to apply it on the court. There are a lot of guys in the schoolyards now who have all kinds of natural abilities—good moves—but they don't know how to use them.

I was born in Manhattan and grew up in the South Bronx. My parents broke up when I was thirteen. I was the oldest boy, so that made me sort of the father image. It was a matter of self-pride for me to keep my family together. I learned to go out and work but at the same time have something in my mind that I wanted to do. Then I could be successful. Even if I hadn't become a pro player, I think I would have pursued something.

Living in a project, I was involved in my community center. I played some baseball and touch football, but basketball was the game that I wanted to get involved in. In basketball you don't really need a whole team to practice. I'd have a basketball and play by myself in the schoolyard—really get my moves down, between the legs, some fleet moves to the basket. Or I'd try to be somebody else who I would never be in real life. I tried to emulate Bob Cousy—not his style—but the way he played. Or Lenny Williams; he was left-handed and a small guard in the league. I just liked the way he quarterbacked guys into the offense. He could handle the ball. I would work on my game for hours by myself or in a five- or ten-man game, and I would try to be this other person in my imagination. I think a lot of kids like me have the dream of becoming some important person in life. I think this kept me off the streets and helped to teach me self-pride.

Some of the guys I grew up with were better than me; some weren't. Those who didn't go to school, I think, had their chances knocked out; the others went to school but eventually dropped out.

Playing in the schoolyards, I might have had the natural talents with my moves and dribbles but I didn't know how to perform them on the basketball court. It took a coach like Cousy and some of the older guys I grew up with to make me see this. A guy may have the ability but sometimes he overuses it or doesn't use it at all. Cousy taught me more about the game of basketball than anyone—handling the ball, running the team, being more of a quarterback and not really a scorer. I felt he didn't really care who did the scoring. I was a good ball handler and I did some of the tricks he did back when he was playing. I think this is why he took it upon himself to teach me more about the game than probably anybody else on our team.

The more I played, the more confidence I built in myself, and I just went out there and played. When I was a youngster the images I had created carried me forward. Then came the reality. I played Lenny Wilkins, Jerry West, Oscar Robertson. I had to remember what Cousy told me. Try to keep my head up and just see those guys cutting and slashing—just see where they are on the floor. You have to realize what kind of guys you're playing with. In time basketball becomes more and more of an instinct game. It's not a planned thing where you have to pass the ball all the time, because a lot of players are not good passers. It's something that you see—guys cutting and moving in. You see them at the last split second, and to be a good ball handler you have to realize that one guy's open so you try to pass him the ball the best possible way. Whether it's behind your back, between the legs, a flick of the wrist, over the head or whatever, try to have the whole vision of the floor. Just to see these guys playing and being able to play against them! I'd seen what they could do and maybe they could do it to me, so I'd better bring my best stuff in there. It was an experience I don't have words to explain. I was very excited, very excited.

The dream was just to play—to emulate someone's style and to play against them. The dream came true when I did get a chance to play. Now

I'd like to fulfill another dream that I have. After my playing days are over, I'd like to do a lot of recruiting around the United States and get a bunch of kids who have been cast off or put aside and see if they are coachable. And hopefully, to win a championship.

I was involved with a lot of kids when I was a senior in high school, and I still work in a lot of summer basketball programs. I try to get back to the projects when I have a chance. There are lots of reasons why I get involved with kids. I was a kid myself and I felt and still feel the disadvantages of my family not being complete. Some of these kids don't have fathers or their living conditions are all wrong. I try to deal creatively with the kids and give my all because I know what it's like for a guy like me or Earl Monroe or Dean Meminger to go back to their neighborhoods and talk to a handful of kids. Kids like to test you; they're always trying to call you out saying, "I want a piece of you." I think it's good. I try by my own moves and creativity to fool them, throw them off balance, make them commit themselves, so one of them can see the easy shot.

The center we play in has twelve teams, eight kids on each team. A lot of kids don't play on a team so we open the center at night and have scrimmages. We get a lot of kids, especially then, because they don't have anything else to do. They play until they get tired and go home or they just hang out and talk about their experiences at the center. I think that's nice.

Since I have more experience, I try to be creative with the kids off the court as well as on it. I try to tell them things in their best interest. Some kids say, "I just want to be you, trade places for a little while, get your money, and just have fun. I think I'm better than you now." I like to tell them the truth. Maybe they're not going all the way to being a pro. Their abilities may carry them over but then they may not. I came up; it was hard for me, and I'm not just going to give it up and pass it on just like that. I don't have anything to do with their success. Only they do. It might be hard for them, but then again it might be easy. But if they're dedicated and work at it, then maybe their chances are good. Right now, I tell them, there's nothing free out there. You have to work for everything you get. I feel that way about myself. If you don't feel like playing, sit down or don't even show up.

I like to share my dreams. I like to give other people the chance to get involved in the game like I did. This is the chance I want to give the youngsters—the chance to get an education and learn something about basketball. Hopefully, they'll go in the right direction. Maybe some of them will become professionals. I think some of them will become men.

Pete Maravich

Everything I know about basketball I learned from my father. I like to think that he made sort of a robot out of me, sort of a bionic person, because of what he wanted. I'm not ashamed of that. He was instrumental in making me what I am today. Actually, you might say I was born with a basketball, because in early baby pictures I had one of the first basketballs made with the strings tied to it, and my daddy put it in the crib with me. That was like an omen for Pete Maravich.

I actually started playing basketball when I was four years old. We lived in Pennsylvania and we had a small goal out back. My dad, who was a high school coach at the time, would go out back and shoot, just fooling around. I'd be inside playing with my toys. One day I went out like any little kid does. I wanted to shoot. "Let me shoot." And he said, "No, get away." So I went back inside the house to my mother and said, "He won't let me shoot." She said, "Don't worry about it." I kept going and he kept pushing me away. Finally a week later he said, "Okay. I'll let you take one shot." There was no way I could get the ball through the basket, of course, but I just kind of threw it up. He said, "Okay, go back inside." and I went back inside and cried again. What he had done was just bait me. He baited me so well that from that point on I just wanted to play basketball.

We moved to South Carolina when I was eight years old. I was dedicated to the game. It was intensity through and through. I knew nothing else; nothing else existed. I was a very unusual child at the time. My interests were solely directed. I played eight or nine hours a day. I went to sleep with a basketball in my bed. The only other things I did were to eat and to drink water and consume necessary nutrients for my body. I got teased quite a bit, especially from my friends. They'd say, "You don't want to go with us?" "You want to come up here? So-and-so is having a little party." "No. I've got to play."

There was a YMCA I used to go to by myself. It was closed on Sundays and I used to sneak in the window. I played in a very small, cold gym about half the size of a regular court. I used to do things that my father taught me. I wanted to be able to do everything with a basketball that was humanly possible. I continually excelled at what I did and would

make things more and more difficult for myself. I just stayed in that gym, though I was scared to death. I was always scared that the bogey man was there, that he was going to get me. I'd hear all kinds of strange noises and I was always alert, aware, wondering if I should shoot, wondering if he was looking at me. I guess I was strange. When you're alone like that you do things that you can never do when somebody else is around. I can't do things now that I did at age nine. Once I got into organized basketball, the circus type performance I used to put on left me—obviously, for what I'm doing now.

When I was in junior high school I was 5 feet 10 and 150 pounds, and when I was a senior I was 6 feet 4 and 150 pounds. Most kids who grow that fast become very clumsy. The thing that saved me was that my father worked out a routine called homework basketball—handling the coordination, the dribbling aspects, and so forth. I was doing so many different things with the basketball from a coordination point of view that it didn't affect me when I grew those 6 inches so quickly.

Until I was fifteen or sixteen all my fantasies were basketball related. School was so boring for me. I knew I had to go there to get where I wanted to later on, but I'd just sit and count off the minutes. I just wanted to play basketball and make a living and that was that. Throughout my life I kept a C average and when I finally left LSU, eleven hours short of a degree, I was about 2.6 on a 4, which isn't too bad. But I didn't push myself. I majored in business, but I wish I had majored in theater or radio broadcasting. Now I kick myself in the behind, but at the time I was obsessed with surviving so I said, well, I'll just major in business. Maybe way deep in the back of my mind I didn't want to be caught up in something that would take me away from basketball. I didn't want to take a chance on becoming interested in something else. Once I realized what pro ball money was all about—I saw the figures when I was sixteen, seventeen—I said, well, that scale will keep going up and it's going to be phenomenal. If I'm good at what I'm going to do, I'll make a lot of money and be able to live my life the way I want to live it with my family and that will be that. It came true.

My dad didn't push me. I pushed myself. When I was very young I *couldn't understand anything. As I said, it was like being a robot. But that was when I was still very young. I just went on. I was extraordinary from that point of view. My father is such a genius in the strategy and philosophy of basketball that it's unbelievable. Without his teaching methods I would never have gotten where I am now. When they get older, most kids rebel against their parents and say, "You pushed me into this. I didn't want to do that. . . ." I don't know, I guess it's a different trip for different folks. It was extraordinary that I began to push myself.*

There are a lot of important aspects to being a player in any sport. Number one is winning. Number two is the fans who are important because without them there is no basketball, football or baseball, no entertainment. Number three, I think, is somehow putting together winning and entertaining people. I've always entertained the fans. That's mostly what I did in college. I very much enjoyed doing a particular thing on the court that I knew would get a standing ovation. It would get our team off. There was such enthusiasm that it would change the momentum of the game. A certain little play and all of a sudden the fans would go haywire.

When I was growing up I worked on this entertainment aspect. I'd say to myself, you're doing things for basketball nobody else is doing. Nobody. Now, for instance, when I play in L.A. I fantasize about really doing things that are out of the ordinary. But I don't do them just to do them; I can't. For example, if I'm coming down on a fast break and there's a guy on my right side and you're a defensive goal and I throw the ball over to him, I'm telegraphing my thoughts. You may see it, so I have to do something deceptive. It might be artistic, but it's got to be deceptive. I might come down, fake, and throw it over there. I might throw it between my legs, behind my back—something that will not only make the crowd go crazy, but that will make 2 points. Coming out on the court is a tremendous high, but the most tremendous high is winning. And I've never really been associated with a winning team in basketball. That's not particularly Pete Maravich's fault, because you're not always geographically where you want to be. You'll say, "Oh. I want to go to Boston, thank you. I'll go to L.A. to see Kareem Jabbar." I'd become a winner instantly, but then I wouldn't know what the other side of the coin was.

Growing up I thought that you had to win, win, win. Win everything. I'd win downing my milk. I'd beat my brother downing my milk. It's really strange, but I was just that competitive. Just playing pool, Ping-Pong, or anything, I'd want to win. It's not that I'm out for the other guy. It could be my brother Ronnie I'm playing with. I want to win. I know he feels the same way; he wants to beat me just to show, hey, see that? I beat you. It really doesn't mean anything.

Although I've only been on one winning team in my seven years, I feel very fortunate for what I've gone through—learning to handle the criticism, just getting older, growing up, experimenting, relating to different people. I feel very comfortable now. I think it's good to lose if you can cope with it. It can do strange things to you. It used to do strange things to me, but now I can cope with it.

I knew my abilities and that it would be just a matter of time before they would start to show. Of course, I could get injured tomorrow, and for the rest of my life that would be it. If I play the rest of my career, say another seven years making fourteen, fifteen years in all, about two years later I'll suddenly be about eighty. But that's something that I've never really dealt with for this reason: I'm not the type of person who says, "Well, one day it's all going to end, and that's it." One aspect of my life is going to end. I hope before that aspect ends—and it could end quicker than you think if I were to win a world championship or be on a team that won a world championship, because I would quit, I'd automatically quit—I would have achieved what I've been working for my entire life. All I want is to achieve the highest level that I can in basketball. There is no other level. The only thing left would be to be declared world champion at what I do. For that one day, for that one moment, you are the best at what you do. That would be the ultimate for me in the first thirty-odd years or so of my life. Not the money, not the joy or the personal achievement. Personal achievements mean nothing to me, because I always knew that from the time I dedicated myself to playing I would always have personal achievements. So that became secondary. I have a fear of quitting without attaining the championship. That's the only thing that keeps me going. I'd be totally crushed, I really would. Totally crushed. I'd come out of it, but it wouldn't be the same thing. I really

don't know. I hope it doesn't happen. I hope I get what I want. That's the ultimate.

I don't want to be misleading. What I used to love and dedicate myself to is no more. I don't love this game anymore. Sports is a flesh-peddling business. It's a very cold business. I've seen guys traded on airplanes. Guys go to lockers and there's another guy's uniform in that locker. It's a very cold situation. You don't have that much time in what you're doing and you don't know what you're going to do for a living, and all of a sudden you're dropped down to earth. Nobody out there is going to help you. They all jump on the bandwagon and then they all jump off. I have so many things that I want to accomplish in what I call my other lives on earth. If I get my championship by the time I'm thirty-four years old, the first thirty-four years of my life will have been totally worth it. That will make up for all the bad things that have happened to me during my lifetime—everything. What I will have done those thirty-four years is to play basketball, and that's it.

From the money standpoint I'm fairly well secure. I think if I want to live my life-style I could probably live forty-five years, which would put me close to sixty something. Then I'd be broke. So maybe I'm not secure from that standpoint; maybe I would want to come back. I'd better get some more money. I've got my chance now to go for security. I play because it's my living and I have something to obtain from it—but other than that, no way. I don't love the game.

I thrive on pressure situations. I love them. Winning or losing, I win. I'll take the blame. I'll take the good things that go with it. I really will. I give myself time to do the job that I'm expected to do. Most nights, say seven out of ten, I do the job. Three of those nights I don't. I used to abuse myself terribly but I don't do it anymore. Like I said earlier, I've learned to cope with it. I think that had a lot to do with growing older and putting myself in perspective. One person doesn't win every basketball game and one person doesn't lose every basketball game. So what makes me happy about it now? Just one thing, looking forward to maybe breaking out the champagne bottles. Some day I'll drive myself toward another ambition. I've lived, what, a third or half my life by American standards. I feel like I'll live to be a hundred, but doesn't everybody?

Bob McAdoo

My confidence is almost full-fledged right now. I think that's the secret. If you don't have confidence, I don't think you're going to be a good player. You need a lot of determination, too. You almost have to be cocky. You know you're going to beat the man you're playing. You know you're going to stop him when he comes on defense. I'm determined I'm going to get out there and nobody is going to stop me. I think I've had it lucky, too, because I didn't get a lot of publicity. I've noticed that a lot of young guys who get a lot of publicity or are supposed to the best or are constantly compared to other great players, start early to be under pressure. I don't think a young guy can handle that pressure. I kind of sneaked up. Everybody was shocked and surprised. I wasn't. I knew that I could do it and that's how I liked it.

New York City is the place every athlete wants to go. I'd never really thought about it, so I don't feel any pressure here. I was starting to feel pressure in Buffalo. I'd hit 30 or 40 points and people would say, "That's a regular McAdoo game." They didn't realize it takes a lot of concentration to do that; they were just taking me for granted. That was pressure to me. I was expected to do that well every night. People didn't know that it was hell. They just expected me to hit my 30. That's not needed here in New York. I think my career will last longer like this. I think I would probably have burned myself out in Buffalo.

I play because I enjoy the game. I like that feeling of putting the ball in the hoop. You're so good you just keep putting them in the basket. You keep on doing that and you can see the other guy getting discouraged, putting his head down. I've seen that a lot. I like that, making a guy put his head down.

I take out a lot of my frustrations on the court. I do it purposely to keep myself up. Statistically, I've done everything. I don't think I can do better. It's frustrating to me because I've improved every year of my professional life, but I haven't won an NBA championship.

Basketball wasn't my main sport when I was growing up. I was a football and baseball player. Then about seventh or eighth grade my height started taking off. I was four or five inches taller than other guys, so basketball came naturally to me. I played better than most of the guys I was

playing against. I was the only one who could dunk the ball. That got me really excited.

My ambition wasn't really in sports. I guess you could say it was in my relationship to my peer group. Everybody was into sports when I got to junior high school. All the guys I hung around with were into athletics and I just followed right along behind them. I really loved football and baseball; basketball was the last sport I got into.

I just loved the hitting in football. I was a wild person then and I showed more feeling out on the football field than I could in any other sport. I was taller than most guys, I was fast, I was good—the perfect split end. But I kept on getting hurt because I was thin. I thought I could be best at football but my build was getting better for basketball. I saw they could double-team you on the football field and they could stop you, so I started concentrating on basketball. On a basketball court it was mostly one on one play and there was no way that I was going to let anybody stop me one on one. That's the philosophy that I brought from the seventh and eighth grade up to now.

When college recruiters started scouting me, I knew that basketball was my sport. I chose to go to a junior college. I had the necessary C+ average to get into a lot of four-year schools, but I wanted to play in the Atlantic Coast Conference. At that time I needed an eight hundred college board score and I didn't get it, so I went to a junior college with the idea of transferring out in one year. It happened we won the national championship that first year, so I decided to stay the next year and play with a lot of good talent. We had a full team of all stars. I played in the Pan-American games after my sophomore year, so I had another chance to play against a lot of good players. I was the only junior college player out of the seventy that made the team, so that was a big thrill for me right there. When I was invited to the games I was skeptical about going, because I had seen all those guys playing on TV. I said to myself, they're playing at these larger schools and I'm playing at a junior level. Will I be able to compete? But I went out there and it was a breeze. I think that I was so psyched up that I ran through the trials. At that point, right there, I got my confidence up. I knew that I could play the game. After that sum-

mer I enrolled in North Carolina and we were either number one or number two the whole year. We went all the way to the semifinals and got beat by Florida State. Pro scouts were after me really heavy and I decided to leave. I had my hardships and they accepted it.

I've been very close to my family. My mother is a schoolteacher and she's very big on the education thing. She was hurt when I told her I was going hardship. I told her that it was something that I had to do. My father was a cop. He was disabled and getting a social security check of about sixty-seven dollars a month. We weren't a poor family; we were like a middle-class black family. But there were things I wanted. I realized basketball was the quickest way to get them. My father told me from the beginning that it was my decision. My mother was uptight. She said, "You can always play pro ball. It will be there. But you can't play it forever." We used to get into little arguments. I told her, "Finishing school is not going to get me good money and that's what you go to school for, to get yourself a better job. What's the need for a degree when I'm going to play professional ball anyway. I can't use the degree for that. If something happens I can always go back to school." So she was finally won over. I think I was sort of waiting for her to turn my way.

That first year with the Braves was the most frustrating year in my whole life because we played eighty-two games, but I didn't really start playing till about the end of December. At that time I must have been averaging about 8 points a game but by will I ended up strong and averaged 18 points, 12 rebounds. I got the award for rookie of the year. I guess that was about the only satisfying thing that year because we lost the season. Next year they traded a lot of guys. Randy Smith moved from forward to guard and he came into his own. We really jelled as a team. That second year they brought in better players and that made me a better player. But I'd say for me there was a little bit of luck, too. I got on a team that had a lot of young players and I got a chance to play right away and to develop. A lot of guys just come on established teams and it takes years for them to develop.

One of the reasons I left the University of North Carolina was that the university was making money off me and it was time for me to make

money off me. I play because I love the game and because it gives me a better life than I had. I've dreamed more about having a better life than I have of being a better basketball player. If I do get my eleven or twelve years in, my salary is going to jump up tremendously. I just don't want to go back to where I was. That's my main concern now. Now I'm playing ball better than I thought I could and I have a beautiful family and just consider myself a lucky person. I put a lot of effort into it too, but I also think it's been a lot of luck. I think I made good decisions during my life. I went to the right junior college. Out of thousands in this country, ours ended up winning the national championship. I went to the right university, the University of North Carolina, and had a great coach, Dean Smith. He taught me about basketball and about life. After my first years in the pros I started saying to myself, I wish I had stayed in school. But when I look back on it, well, so far it's come out perfect.

Julius Erving

Duthe baseball season everybody played baseball; during the football season, football; and during the basketball season, basketball. It was a neighborhood thing and a matter of following the seasons. Although I was successful at basketball from the time I started playing at eight or nine, I wasn't looking at it in terms of making it my livelihood. No way! We played strictly unorganized, just for the fun of it. Somebody would say, "Let's choose up sides and play basketball." Could be football or baseball; there was always a consistency with the seasons.

The park near where I lived was built around 1961 when I was eleven, and then things became a little more structured. But I still remained diversified until my senior year in high school. That's when I gave up all other sports. I had a stronger feeling for basketball. I'd seen a couple of pro games by then and I admired it. I preferred the basketball season to all the other seasons. But there was no way that I dedicated myself at that time to becoming a pro. Not consciously. I just loved to do it. Subconsciously I might have put more work hours into it than I realized. There was a combination of physical and emotional satisfaction in playing. There was great intensity in basketball that I didn't feel when I played football or baseball. Basketball combines finesse with physicality and for me it had a certain feeling that was different from the other sports. I also related to it better, maybe because of the way I was built. I was thin and fast and had good jumping ability, so basketball was natural.

It became a truly enjoyable thing for me. If certain things troubled me or there was some conflict at home, I could take my ball, go out to the park, and play by myself for a few hours and it would make the whole situation pass by. I wouldn't be uptight any more. It would really cool me out. I'd work up a good sweat, get a quart of orange juice, sip it, and suddenly it was utopia. There's a certain degree of fantasizing I can recall, imitating pro players that I'd heard about or seen: Oscar Robertson, Wilt Chamberlain, Jerry West—or whoever the premier players in the pros were. Sometimes I'd go out on the court and shoot a shot and say somebody's name as though imitating their shot or their game, putting myself in their place, maybe hoping that one day I could be there.

I first started playing organized basketball with the team from the Salvation Army in Hempstead. The coach, Don Ryan, was really a young adult, nineteen years old. He emphasized that if we wanted to be on the team we had to be gentlemen, because we were representing our town. We went to different places around Long Island. We were sent to the city to play and to Philadelphia. One of the things that you had to observe to be on the team was that your conduct was as important as how well you played basketball. If we wanted to play, there were certain standards that we had to live up to. We had to bring our report cards to him, too. I thought he was right. It was the same thing once I started playing for the school team. All the teachers felt the same way, so it was something I started to believe in.

In high school I played because I enjoyed it. I had school spirit and team spirit. When I played I represented my school, that was what was happening. After my junior year in high school, the seniors on the team had college scouts come and look at them, and a couple of them were offered scholarships. In my own mind I felt I was just as good or better than they were, or that I had more to offer a college. Before that my perspective was narrow, it was in the present. I didn't know what was going to happen the next year. I wasn't rushing things—although in later years my tendency was to start streaking a little bit.

Well, I had a lot of scouts who saw me play and wanted me to come and visit a million and one schools. Many times when I went to the different schools other high school players were there too, guys who had done the same things I had done in high school. I found that the programs had a hard sell to them. They made a lot of promises to everybody. I was kind of an in-between size then, too—about 6 feet 3. If I didn't grow, I might have to be a guard. I was used to playing forward, playing close to the basket. I wanted to play forward for whatever school I was going to go to. I decided on Massachusetts because if I was going to develop athletically to fit into that program, I would be given the time. It wouldn't be such a competitive atmosphere where ten guys would receive scholarships and whoever developed first would be out there while the other guys would be jerked around. The academic rating was very high, like a step below

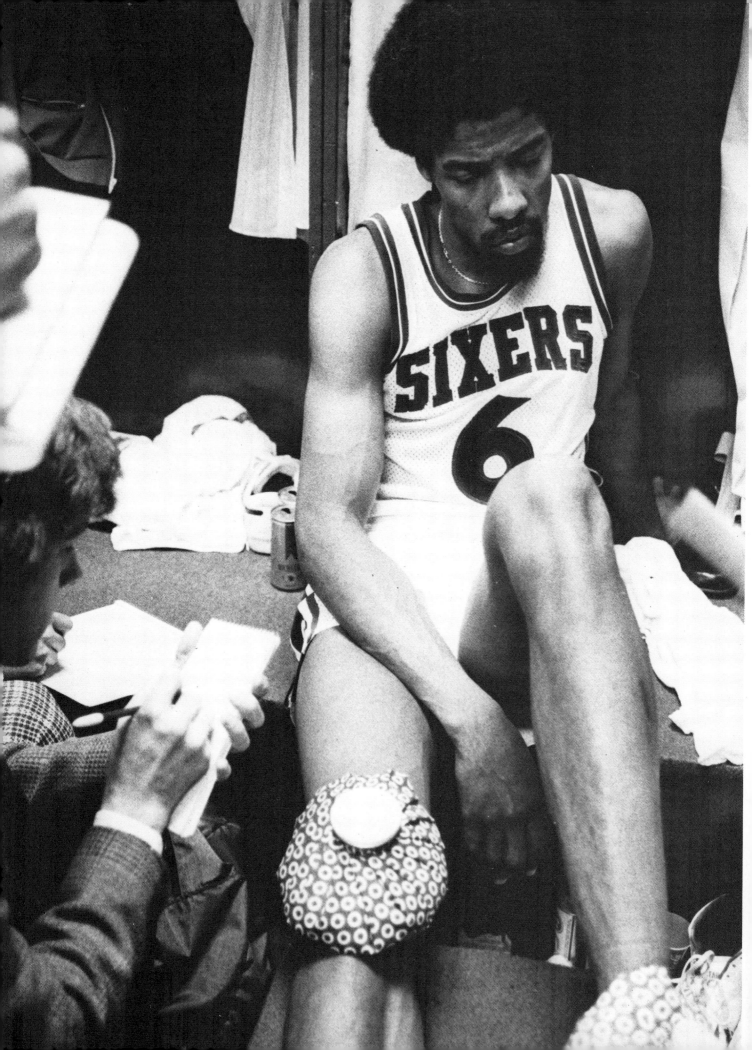

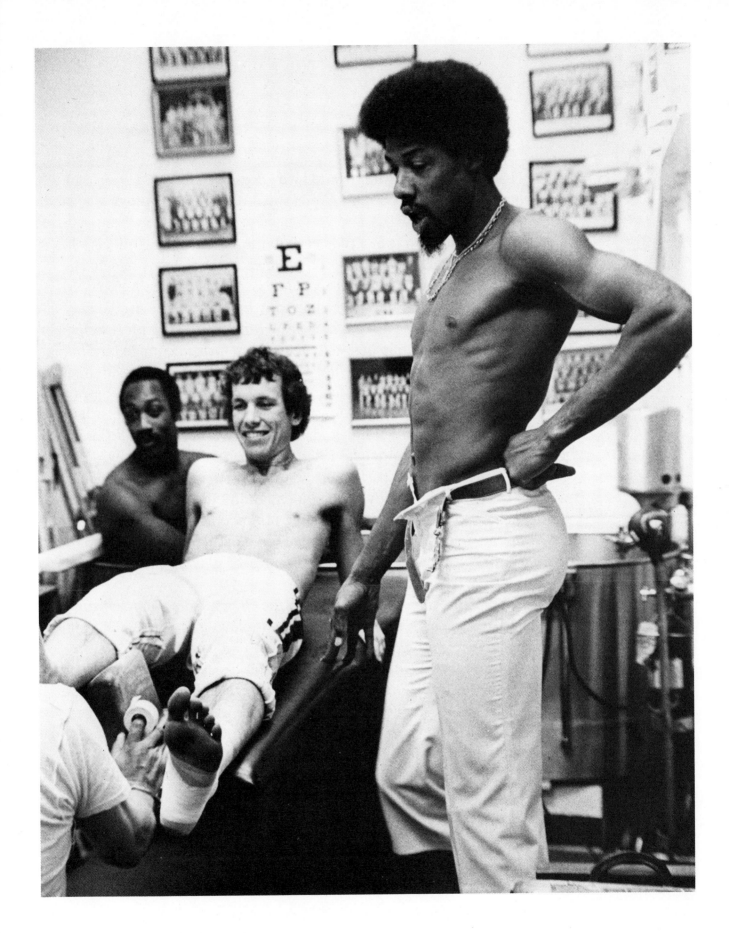

the Ivy League. So I thought it would be a good place for me. I wasn't going to put all my eggs in one basket and say, "Well, I'm going to be a basketball player and that's it."

After my sophomore year I played with all the best young players in the country. I was as good or better than most of them. I was selected as one of the top ten sophomores in the country. That's when I felt I could become a pro. In high school I was basically a scorer but I wasn't a very good shooter. There was always a desire within me to strain for perfection, and the coach I had in high school was very instrumental in pushing me. I wanted to reach my potential and come as close to perfection as possible. My high school and college coaches had a personal relationship with each other and that carried over to me. My high school coach had me improve on my timing and jumping ability. I worked on different drills before and after practice. I had to work constantly—slowly but surely—to strive for that perfection. When I was a freshman in college we played against the varsity team, which I didn't think had players any more talented than I. As a matter of fact, I think our freshman team was much more talented and that reinforced my confidence. But even so, it wasn't until the following year that the idea of playing professionally became a factor in my life.

After competing on a national level in the Olympic development summer camp, a lot of guys started talking about playing pro and what kind of contracts they were going to ask for. It was really beyond me. I hadn't thought about it. Basically I just listened and checked it out, and I remember the figures they were talking about. I remember those conversations. I just thought about the fact that I had two more years to play in college and I was going to have fun playing and that was going to be it. But after that year I knew that I was as good as any young player in the country. When the time came I would probably be drafted—by whom, or what I would be offered, I didn't know. But I really didn't care about it. I dedicated myself to perfecting my skills, and whatever that lead to was a question mark. I've always had a reluctance to commit myself unless it's something that I've initiated.

Julius Erving

It wasn't until concrete offers with guarantees were being made that I sat down and evaluated what my options were going to be. Before that, getting my bachelor's degree in personal management was my number one priority. Once I did accept that professional contract, basketball became my number one priority. I just feel that whatever formula you apply to your life, it should be one that enables you to maintain consistency, and I'm kind of a fiend about consistency. I just sit by myself and evaluate my situation, what I'm doing, where I'm going. Is that what I want? What's happening with my time? What's happening with my life? Am I practicing what I preach? Am I preaching what I practice? Ever since I started doing that I've found that things have fallen into place nicely. It's something I do quite often. I think that it's one of the keys to having a successful life.

On the court I try to stay away from the peaks and valleys. When I come out on court, whatever has happened prior to that, or whatever will happen afterwards, can't affect my performance. I want to try and keep my concentration on an even keel. There are built-in distractions at a game. I find if I have to think about concentrating on the game, that's admitting I've lost it. If you can minimize that, then you can be much more effective. Basketball is entertainment. It competes for the entertainment dollar. People have paid to see me perform. I perform and want to do well for them, but also for myself, for my own pride and desire. Although the primary object of doing anything on the court should be for its result, not its effect, I think the effect is a factor. The effect excites the fans more, and the result pleases the player, because if the result is positive, you get reinforcement from that. Yet if you do something and its effect is great but the result doesn't lead to something that's going to help your team, then it's like, "Nice try buddy, maybe next time." You don't feel good about it. I can go out and dance and jump around, but if we don't score any baskets that's not basketball.

The tendency is for players to want to extend themselves. There are certain times when a team can go out and play a completely free-lance game. Everything they do is spectacular and really exciting. But in the

long run, a team that's disciplined and patterned can beat them. Actually a team that has less talent but more cohesion and unity and is better at executing their stuff can beat a team that's more talented but undisciplined. Sometimes the level of judgment or discretion is very low in a player's mind when he comes down the court. Maybe he sees a one on three situation and decides it's a chance for him to express himself. He's so confident of his ability he feels he can beat them. A player who is less talented would come down one on three or one on two and say, "Okay, I've got two guys back, I'm going to pull the ball back out and wait for some help." Now a player with more talent might come down and say, "Okay, maybe I could split these guys." Actually, he doesn't say it, he just does it. That's a matter of judgment. So the more talent you have, the greater your tendency to be less discreet than the player with less talent.

It's a matter of using the skills that you've developed. I know I can use the skills that I've developed, even though I might not have practiced them for years. At a certain time I know I will use them again. So I build up a whole repertoire of things that I know I can do, and some nights a situation calls for using them and other nights it doesn't. You keep them in storage. The more stuff that you have stored up in your mind or your imagination that you have worked on perfecting, the more versatile, the more creative you'll be on a given night. That's what separates players. When you blend great talent and great judgment in one player, then you have a winner. Those are the guys who are the real winners. Winning is the main objective and everything else comes after that. So if you win and you know you had a super night, then you're very satisfied.

I love my work. I think I have the best job of anybody I know. But I don't like to be related to just as a basketball player, because that's what I do as opposed to what I am. I am a man and being a basketball player is what I do for a living. It's a very big part of my life. It's my livelihood and my profession. But too many times people are judged by their profession alone, especially by people who don't know them. One thing my coach Ray Wilson, who was a very influential person in my life, said, "Never get carried away with yourself so that you start to believe that you're something that you really aren't." The best thing you can do as far as preserving your image is to be something that you actually believe in and that is really you.

If someone tried to guess my personality by seeing me play, they would probably guess wrong. My playing style is a lot different from how I talk and move off the court. The only thing that is similar is the intensity and the concentration level. I usually think about things awhile before I talk about them. On the court I have that type of concentration, but there is a difference, because on the court the game is action versus reaction. I think I play faster. People who are close to me judge me by what I say and what I think.

I have a very basic philosophy about life. My priority list has changed. I don't just think in the present tense as I once did when I was in college or high school. Now I'm planning ahead because I have more responsibilities. With those responsibilities you need advance planning. I think I could have anything I've dreamed about except for one thing I lost. That was when my brother died. That was the worst I've been hurt in my life. Having him back is something I've visualized in dreams, but that's the only way I can have it. I realize that, but it has helped to shape and mold me as a person, too. I got a lot of strength out of that catastrophe and a lot of purpose, and I really settled down into the person I am now. Other than that, there's nothing else that I've dreamed about or wished for that I can't have.

David Thompson

In North Carolina, college basketball was really big. I used to watch all the ACC teams on TV. I always wanted to play on one of the big four teams, and I would envision myself in an ACC championship game down by 1 point, reaching for the ball, taking the last shot, winning. I started to play basketball when I was about seven years old. I was taught primarily by my older brother who played high school basketball. I played in the backyard with him because there wasn't any organized basketball for younger kids. I first played organized basketball when I was in the ninth grade on the junior varsity team and I did pretty well. So for the rest of the year I was asked to move to the varsity tournament, and in my sophomore year I played on the varsity team.

I was thirteen and 6-foot 2, and I knew that my abilities were much better than most of the guys my age. I felt that there was a good chance I'd get taller and I could develop my game more. In my junior and senior years in high school I played a lot with professional players who would come into school now and then. I saw that with a little work I could reach their level. I gained a lot of confidence through those great college and pro players. Every time I played with them they seemed pretty impressed and that gave me even more incentive to work harder. Also, the first couple of years our team wasn't very successful and losing drove me to work more. Everybody wants to be the best, so I put out that much more effort to prove my abilities. I thought I had potential but I knew I had a lot of work to do. When I became a collegiate player and felt it could possibly be within my reach, my dreams stepped up to thoughts of being a professional man.

I wanted to do something for my family and when I got a chance to play professionally, this made me work a little harder still. I was the youngest of eleven kids. I have seven sisters and three brothers. My father was a deacon. He is a very religious man and was pretty strict. My parents lived the right way, but they also had to struggle quite a bit. They really worked their fingers to the bone. I take my having success as part of the reward for all the hard times they had. I do as much for them as I do for myself. Probably more. We're really close. We keep close contact

with each other. I think my parents influence me more than anyone. They've had the greatest influence over the type of person I am.

I like challenges. When I was in high school my idol was Charlie Scott, who played at the University of North Carolina. I saw myself as being the same type of player—the guy that everybody looked for in the clutch. When they needed a basket he was always there to provide it. I wanted to be that type of player. Through the years I picked up a little bit of stuff that I felt would be relevant to my particular game from quite a few players. Erving—watching him play when I was in college—he's like an idol of mine. The thing about Doc is his hand is so big and he's so fluid and does everything so smoothly, it's almost like he's playing effortlessly while doing things that are very difficult. He makes them look easy. Not only does he do things that are unbelievable but he might do six or seven of them in one ball game. I picked up some stuff from him. I think sometimes I do things that are extraordinary. People aren't used to seeing a guy 6-foot 4 make a move and go for a guy.

I have my own particular style and I don't play exactly like any other player. Sometimes I take off, and it just happens. I don't have any preconceived idea of what I'm going to do but I do something spectacular, maybe move around fast and dunk the ball in. I don't know I'm doing it; it just occurs. It's natural. Now I just have to play that much harder because people expect me to come out and play well. That's a big challenge.

I used to challenge my brother when we were playing ball. Sometimes we warred and I would really try to beat him. To achieve, to prove that I was better than that particular guy there—that motivates anyone. I wanted to be the best and I forced myself, drove myself, did extra work in the summers, extra running at the practices, and things like that. In college I was working to have my team be a national championship team. That was always my goal—to be a champion. To be associated with a championship. Winning is definitely important to me. I think that everyone has that desire, that drive to be the best.